This unique book proves just how basic Conservatism has been to the American political scene from the American Revolution and the Birth of the Republic to the present. It indicates just how far Conservatism has come toward its goals and where it is likely to go in the near future.

It sets forth the Conservative stand on such controversial and important issues of the Sixties as:

Bigger (and better!) Federal Government
Civil Liberties and Rights
Communism
Creeping Socialism
Foreign Aid and Policy
Medicare
Parochial School Aid
Social Security and Taxes

and a host of others.

Here is a candid analysis-in-depth of the beliefs and principles of Conservatism, carefully documented by the public speeches, writings and opinions of the leading spokesmen for the Conservative philosophy.

AVON BOOK DIVISION
The Hearst Corporation
572 Madison Avenue
New York 22, N. Y.

CONSERVATISM:
A Guide to its Past, Present and Future in American Politics

Dean Smith

Introduction by
SENATOR BARRY GOLDWATER

To Betty, who was patient

Table of Contents

ACKNOWLEDGMENTS

The political positions of Conservative spokesmen are set forth with clarity in their public addresses, in their writings and in their informal newsletters to constituents. Conservative leaders in both the United States Senate and House of Representatives were most cooperative in making available to the author voluminous material in all three categories. Of particular value were the documents provided by Senators Barry Goldwater of Arizona, Karl Mundt of South Dakota, Harry Byrd of Virginia, Strom Thurmond of South Carolina, John Tower of Texas, and Representatives Charles Halleck of Indiana and John Rhodes of Arizona.

The author also is indebted to Rob Wood of the Associated Press for help in the preparation of the outline and bibliography; to Dr. Bruce Mason, director of the Bureau of Government Research and head of the Department of Political Science, Arizona State University, and to Dr. Heinz Hink, associate professor of political science, Arizona State University, for lending many books and documents; and to Tony Smith, press secretary to Senator Goldwater, and E. J. Demson, lecturer in business law, Arizona State University, for reading and criticizing the manuscript.

PREFACE

All across America today, there is a new stirring of political consciousness.

Millions of citizens are examining their political beliefs in the light of the problems facing our nation in the critical decade of the 1960s. They are listening with great interest to the arguments put forth in the Great Debate between today's Liberal and Conservative spokesmen, and many are joining that debate on one side or the other.

This book is frankly and unashamedly partisan. It presents Conservative viewpoints and Conservative proposals for action, as stated by those who have advocated these viewpoints and proposals most effectively. It attempts to show the essential consistency and continuity of Conservative positions throughout our nation's history.

In its four principal divisions, this book tries to assess how far the present Conservative movement has progressed—how American Conservatism has developed since the winning of national independence—how Conservatives stand on the controversial issues of the present decade—and where Conservatism is likely to go from here.

There are almost as many shades of Conservative belief as there are individual Conservatives, and for that reason no single book can hope to set forth with finality "what Conservatives believe." But there is a broad enough area of agreement in the declarations of Conservative spokesmen to warrant making some general statements about their positions and goals.

Today's Great Debate is in the best tradition of American democracy. From this collision of basic political philosophies, with all its sound and fury, may emerge more effective and more truly representative programs for solving the complex problems facing America in these times.

DEAN SMITH
Scottsdale, Arizona
June, 1962

vii

INTRODUCTION
By Senator Barry Goldwater

Americans are an unmanageable lot.

Just when it appears that they have been propogandized enough, or scared enough, or subsidized enough to turn over their basic responsibilities to those who claim to know what is best for them—they rebel.

It's enough to turn a government planner's hair gray.

In my ten years as a United States Senator, I have been privileged to talk personally to hundreds of thousands of Americans in every part of our nation. I have watched their rebellion take shape and grow into the Conservative Revival we hear so much about today.

Actually, it is not entirely accurate to call it a "revival," because that term implies regaining something which has been lost. We must remember that most Americans have been essentially conservative since the founding of our country. What is happening today is that millions of them are becoming aware of the dangers which threaten our free institutions and they are beginning to speak out for what they have always believed.

Conservatism offers thought-provoking reading for these newly-aroused conservatives, as well as for all other Americans who are concerned about our nation in this critical decade. For some readers, the points of view this book present will be new and striking. For others, the book will help explain and support positions long espoused. For those whose beliefs are in opposition to those of conservatives, it will offer a standard against which to measure those beliefs.

This book has been written for laymen, by a layman. Dean Smith, who has had experience as a reporter and editor, uses both backgrounds in presenting the viewpoints of selected conservative spokesmen from pre-Constitution days to the present. Among those spokesmen are scholars and practical politicians, Presidents and businessmen, philosophers and reporters on the national scene.

It is interesting to note that, despite the many differences of opinion among conservatives through the years, these spokesmen have been in agreement on basic principles. They all value liberty over security, for example. They believe that power should be diffused. They believe that the marketplace regulates our economy more efficiently than could any government bureau. And they believe that Americans can attain the greatest possible spiritual and material benefits only in a society which guarantees individual freedom of choice.

Today the benefits of these giants of conservatism are being challenged.

I cannot agree with those who tell us that America is now so big and complex that individuals must surrender their rights and responsibilities to an all-powerful central government. I cannot agree that the Constitution is old-fashioned, or that its grants of powers to the states and the people are no longer valid. In short, I cannot believe that we Americans will ever be willing to surrender the management of our lives to a central officialdom which purports to know more about what is good for us than we do.

Conservatives, as this book points out, cannot be content with simple opposition to liberal programs which lead to the monolithic welfare state. We must take a positive approach, developing and advocating programs based on Constitutional principles and dependent for their motive power on individual and community initiative.

The problems which face us today are many and complex and they have been made more numerous and more complex by repeated tampering with the natural laws which have governed the lives of men for thousands of years. But these problems can be solved, and will be solved, when we at last determine to abandon frenzied social experimentation and return to the tested governmental principles which made our nation the greatest the world has ever known.

When can we expect our nation's government to be guided once again by conservative principles?

We can expect that day when the millions of Americans of conservative inclination are motivated enough to discover conservatism, to learn more about it, and to go to work on its behalf.

I believe *Conservatism* may help provide that motivation.

CONSERVATISM.

1.

This Hunger for Freedom

I.

■ TO STAND AND BE COUNTED

There has been nothing quite like it in America before.

On and on the Great Debate of the '60s rages: Liberal! Conservative! In civic gatherings, around neighborhood bars, across powder rooms, on television screens, over brown-bag lunches and fancy hors d'oeuvres, through campus assembly halls and suburban patios it goes on.

Such venerable conversational standbys as sex, religion and baseball are left trailing in its wake.

Sometimes the debaters come armed with bales of facts and figures. More often their arguments are bolstered only by instinctive convictions and the morning newspaper's editorial. Almost without exception the antagonists plead from the heart—from the conviction that the America in which our children will live, if there is to be an America at all, is being unalterably shaped in these crucial days.

Who should be responsible for welfare programs? For education? What about Social Security and the graduated income tax? How much national sovereignty should we surrender to the United Nations? How important are private property rights? Is Senator Byrd right about federal thrift, or is Senator Humphrey? Who should control the Republican Party—the Goldwater or the Rockefeller wing? What about farm subsidies? Compulsory unionism? Federally-enforced integration?

The Great Debate never lacks for subject matter.

But each of the white-hot questions of the day can be reduced to one common denominator: *Individual and community responsibility* vs. *federal responsibility*.

It is the overriding issue of our time, and almost all our courses of action will be determined when that issue is at last decided.

Political debates have flourished in America before, but

usually they have been of shorter duration—principally during the months preceding presidential elections—and usually they have centered on the personalities of the candidates themselves.

But the Great Debate of the '60s runs deeper. It concerns ideas, principles, basic differences in political philosophy: it is the best and healthiest thing that has happened to our nation in many a decade.

That there is a Liberal vs. Conservative debate at all is a tribute to the indestructibility of Conservatism. In the 30 years which have elapsed since Franklin D. Roosevelt launched his New Deal, the nation has been governed by a succession of Liberal administrations dedicated—in varying degrees—to the proposition that the federal government is better able to solve the complex problems of modern America than are individual Americans or their local and state governments.

Only an amazingly hardy political idea—and a basically sound one—could survive such a long period of involuntary retirement and step back into the arena in fighting trim.

Conservatism is just such an idea.

Partisans on both sides of the Great Debate who had hoped for a mammoth demonstration of public endorsement in the November 1962 general elections were doomed to disappointment. Liberals could take cheer in the fact that expected losses in the Congressional races did not materialize. And Conservatives could rest easier in the knowledge that their coalition of Republicans and Conservative Democrats would retain control in the 88th Congress.

"Radicalism is checked again," exulted David Lawrence in his nationally-syndicated newspaper column of November 11, 1962. "All the talk of 'net gains'—by mathematically putting together the Senate and House victories of the Democrats—doesn't alter the fact that it needs only a coalition in one house to block radical legislation. This barrier exists more firmly than ever before against unsound fiscal policies and the proposals which, if enacted, would discourage and retard business progress. Indeed, it would not be surprising if 1964 finds President Kennedy campaigning with a less liberal and more conservative strategy than he followed in 1960."

The election only served to emphasize how evenly divided Americans are today over the basic questions of the Great Debate. And it sounded a warning that extremists on both sides can expect rough going in the years just ahead.

Both the 1962 elections and the second session of the 87th Congress demonstrated conclusively that the Conservative philosophy is here to stay. Even those Liberals who were declaring a few short years ago that the welfare state and further government centralization were being borne on tides of history are now convinced that the American people are not nearly so submissive as they once imagined.

The issue is still very much undecided, and the Great Debate will occupy us for many years to come.

That the long-entrenched opposition philosophy is known as "Liberalism" is ironic. The traditional liberalism of the Western world had for centuries been based on the principle of individual responsibility, and it firmly opposed the centralization of political power.

It would be hard, for example, to imagine the liberal Thomas Jefferson or his ideological descendents supporting a "planned" national economy, cradle-to-grave welfare programs, or a sprawling federal establishment that controls some facet of every American's life a dozen times a day and extracts a third of his income to pay the bill.

"The limitation of government to its proper sphere," wrote Jefferson, "is the essence of republican government, and this limitation comprises as an important element the division of the country into States, the 'true barriers of our liberty'."

But it is not the primary purpose of this book to point up the failures of modern Liberalism. For too many years, Conservatives were content to do little more than that. In their futile grumbling, they failed to come forward with positive programs capable of solving our complex modern problems within the framework of the freedoms which made this nation great.

The time for bemoaning the loss of American freedoms

is past. The time for proclaiming programs which will regain those freedoms is here.

Americans today must check their maps to determine how far we already have traveled down the road to statism, and how much it has cost. We must understand how many of our rights and responsibilities we already have surrendered to the federal government—and decide whether this is the route we want to follow for the rest of the Twentieth Century.

John T. Flynn, in *The Road Ahead*, wrote: "The road we are traveling is sufficiently clear. We cannot delude ourselves with the expectation that we may go a little way further and then stop in the belief that we can combine socialism and capitalism, and preserve the best features of each. The very first hard and cold fact that we must face is that these two systems cannot live together in the same society. . . ."

Clinton Rossiter admirably summed up the need for a re-examination of national direction when he declared in his book *Conservatism in America* that, "The first step toward an alert and responsible conservatism is for several million more 'old-fashioned liberals' to wake up some morning and admit that they have been conservatives all their lives. The conservative must understand what conservatism is, and why it should exist; he must know something of its part in the proper functioning of a free society. The American conservative must discover conservatism."

In these days of decision, Americans of Conservative tendency must be willing to stand and be counted. And they must speak out for their beliefs. To their credit, Liberals have never been hesitant to do so. They have flooded the book shelves, the magazine stands, and the Letters to the Editor columns with their philosophy of centrally-directed action. One of Conservatism's most glaring deficiencies has been in its shortage of articulate spokesmen.

No wonder Conservatives have been on the defensive, convinced they were waging a futile battle against overwhelming numbers. They have simply been out-talked, out-publicized, and out-hustled by the Liberals, who have been willing to take the time and spend the energy necessary to declare their ideas and elect their candidates.

The sheer force of the Liberal campaign has made many a Conservative feel somehow ashamed of his instincts, and led him to be about as willing to express them as would a member of a rough-and-ready gang of 12-year-old boys to admit that he liked ballet.

Senator Barry Goldwater, among whose goals has been that of "making Conservatism once again respectable," has for a decade been urging his fellow Conservatives to come out of the shadows and speak out proudly for their beliefs.

"President Eisenhower announced during his first term, 'I am a conservative when it comes to economic problems but liberal when it comes to human problems,'" wrote Goldwater in his best-selling *Conscience of a Conservative*. "Still other Republican leaders have insisted on calling themselves 'progressive' Conservatives—a strange label which implies that 'ordinary' Conservatism is opposed to progress. Have we forgotten that America made its greatest progress when Conservative principles were honored and preserved?"

Too many people with Conservative instincts, concludes Goldwater, feel compelled to apologize for them.

Yet Conservatives have every reason to stand proudly. Theirs is the tradition which founded America, hammered out the best Constitution the world has ever known, and created the economic climate in which the nation's unmatched productive capacity was built. Conservatism has jealously guarded individual opportunity and freedom, fought the centralization of government power, and has insisted throughout our history that American government be guided by the same principles of financial responsibility which guide family and business operations.

Americans have always been among the most conservative of all the world's people. Convinced of the essential rightness of hard work, individual enterprise, thrift, and reverence for the laws of God and the lessons of history, Americans for generations have lived the principles of Conservatism.

How, then, did it come about that the very name of Conservatism fell into disrepute?

For a combination of reasons. Among them were: (1) the forces of economic boom and bust which swept across the world after World War I, (2) the failures exhibited by Conservative American business and political leadership in meeting the challenges of both prosperity and depression in those fateful 12 years, and (3) the success enjoyed by Liberals in their efforts to discredit Conservatism in the wake of those failures.

In the panic and disillusionment of the early 1930s, too many Americans forgot all about the solid successes of Conservative principles which had guided most national administrations as far back as Washington's. The proven ways suddenly became old-fashioned, and the nation was ready to submit to almost any kind of experimentation and regimentation if it offered hope of economic security.

It was during that time of upheaval that vocal Liberals were able to establish a vivid, but highly distorted, image of the Conservative. In the Liberal view, he was a selfish, bloated, tight-fisted money worshiper; a foe of social progress and a scorner of the working man; a stodgy foot-dragger who looked longingly backward and refused to admit that times had changed.

Liberals still insist, says William F. Buckley, in *Up From Liberalism*, that Conservatism is either a product of unbalanced mentality or "a lowering political force that threatens to ring in a new Dark Age."

What have Conservatives done to present their philosophy as it really is? Until recently, not very much. A few on the radical fringe have resorted to the same Liberal techniques of distortion and name-calling. To them, all Liberals are "pinks," if not outright Communists. College professors and the Protestant clergy are subversive. Recent presidents in both parties were treasonous.

Such declarations, from either the right or the left, have no place in the healthy debate of the '60s.

With few exceptions, leaders of both the Liberal and Conservative points of view are sincere, intelligent, loyal Americans.

But somebody is *right* and somebody is *wrong* in this debate.

Conservatives must muster every resource at their command to demonstrate the superiority of their way. The past decade has produced a resurgence of Conservatism, but

Conservatives still have a long way to go. Thirty years of moving toward collectivism will not be overcome by anything less than the concerted efforts of millions of Conservatives to develop better programs for the solution of America's problems—programs which are based on individual initiative rather than reliance on the federal government—and to convince all Americans of their soundness and workability.

The hard facts are these: that Liberals have won millions of converts by providing "something for everyone"—subsidies for some, relief checks for others, price supports here, giveaways there. If all this federal generosity has resulted in staggering taxation, and in a national debt that is beyond comprehension, who complains? Just a few old-fashioned, moss-backed Conservatives. Taxes can be cleverly camouflaged, and the debt is already so huge that, after all, what is another few billion dollars?

Besides, it is all done in the spirit of helping *people*. Who but a man who hates *people* could be opposed to such programs?

So goes the Liberal argument.

But somehow the message must be gotten across: that here is no money tree in Washington—that the only money available for giveaways must come from the American people themselves, or from unborn generations who must some day wrestle with the debt we are piling up today. And that every new giveaway whittles away just a little more of our individual responsibility, encourages a little more inflation, and adds to the growing mountain of federal power.

Peter Drucker, writing in the June 1955 *Harper's*, pointed up the dangers of modern inflationary trends. "Inflation," he said, "is not only an impersonal and general danger to society—the breeder of class hatred and the destroyer of the middle class. In an economy where the great mass of people have become long-term creditors (through insurance and pensions) and where as much as half of the employed population is on fixed salaries which do not readily adjust to changes in money values, inflation may cause more individual suffering than even widespread unemployment. . . ."

Conservatives are opposed to government-financed medical care for the aged? Then let us propose better ways to solve the problems which earlier retirement and longer life have thrust upon us.

Conservatives are against federal grants to the unemployed in technologically depressed areas? Then we must come up with workable plans for helping the jobless to help themselves.

Conservatives are against federal tampering with free enterprise in business? Then let business accept effective self-regulation that will smooth out the ruinous boom-and-bust cycles which brought on Big Government in the first place.

Conservatives, in short, must do more than battle against the fashionable notion that only the federal government can do an effective job in solving the problems of modern America. They must develop better programs, based on individual and community initiative, and then they must sell them to an electorate which has been buying the competitor's product since 1932.

"More Americans must be made to realize that competitive enterprise, civil and religious freedoms, and political freedom are inseparably bound together," wrote H. W. Prentice, Jr., in *Competitive Enterprise vs. Planned Economy,* "and that when one of the three is undermined, all the liberty they now so smugly enjoy will soon be devoured in the maw of dictatorship."

Salesmen for Conservatism are sure to encounter some sales resistance. A whole new generation of Americans has grown up in an atmosphere of federal paternalism and deep-rooted attitudes are not easy to change.

But Conservatism must be sold with enthusiasm and effectiveness if current trends toward statism are to be reversed.

Federal responsibility or individual responsibility? The first road is wider, easier to travel—and leads eventually to national regimentation and bankruptcy. The second road is rockier, more challenging—and leads to the free, productive society which has always been the American ideal.

II.

◼ THIS CONSERVATIVE REVIVAL

"People—and particularly young people—are worried over the 'trend of the times' in which government apparently is rushing headlong into MORE centralization, LESS individual liberty; MORE deficit spending, LESS concern for the taxpayer; MORE circumvention of constitutional government, LESS reliance on tested, workable theories of tripartite government; and MORE secrecy in executive activities, LESS faith in the people to accept responsibility."

The words are those of South Dakota Senator Karl Mundt. The sentiments are shared by most of his fellow Conservatives.

The Conservative Revival which stirred so many millions of Americans into active opposition to the Liberal philosophies of the New Deal and Fair Deal more than a decade ago, and which has fueled the Great Debate of the 1960s, continues to reshape American political thought.

That it has not yet gained the upper hand for Conservatism is evident in the 1962 national elections, which resulted in a virtual standoff instead of the solid gains hoped for by Conservative spokesmen.

What the election showed—in addition to the fact that many people vote for personalities instead of issues—is that America is becoming increasingly moderate. Extremists on both the right and left went down to defeat. But the all-important result in the Conservative view, was that the coalition of Conservative Republicans and Democrats will continue to control Congress through 1964.

It is certain that Conservatism, once believed buried under an avalanche of radical Liberal advances, has regained its determination to preserve individual liberty and responsibility on the domestic front, and American leadership in the world community of nations.

23

Events in the early years of the 1960s prove that the Conservative philosophy appeals to Americans of all ages and of all economic stations. It knows no sectional boundaries, either, although it remains stronger in the Midwest, South and West than in the East—more potent in the small towns and on the farms than in the metropolitan centers.

There could be no more convincing demonstration of America's resurgent Conservatism than the story of the second session of the 87th Congress.

Time and again the Administration stormed the battlements, seeking passage of one expensive piece of federal welfare legislation after another. New Frontier forces pressured and cajoled on behalf of stricter federal regimentation of agriculture, massive federal aid to education, Medicare, a Department of Urban Affairs, and other programs which promised tempting "benefits" at the cost of individual and community initiative.

And each time Congress, despite the Administration party's heavy majorities in both houses, turned back the assault. The nation's legislators, their ears tuned to the expressed desires of the voters back home, were unwilling to send America one step further down the path toward centralized federal power and the Welfare State.

Even the staunchest efforts of Conservatives, however, were unequal to the task of reversing the 30-year trend toward increasing national indebtedness. In March 1962, the debt ceiling was pushed up to $300 billion, and near the end of the session it went to $308 billion. The Fiscal Year 1963 deficit alone reached $8 billion. Built-in spending increases will undoubtedly force further debt extensions in the near future. But had Congress succumbed to New Frontier pressures for additional welfare programs, the debt ceiling might have joined our satellites in outer space.

More dramatic evidence of the Conservative Revival may be found in the almost unanimous national determination to take a firm stand against the Communist menace in Cuba. Radical Liberals had for years insisted that Fidel Castro was a benevolent agrarian reformer, and that America must not risk war by daring to stand fast against the threat his revolutionary Cuban government posed to this nation and its Latin-American neighbors.

Castro's eventual declaration that he and his government had been Communist all along shook the Liberals to their heels, but even then they were unwilling to take positive action against him. Fortunately for the nation, President Kennedy proved to be more of a realist than many of his Liberal advisors, however, and on October 22, 1962, he heartened the entire Free World with his announcement that a "quarantine" had been imposed upon Cuba to enforce removal of Russian missile bases on the island. Aerial reconnaissance photos which revealed the presence of the missile bases at last triggered the action which leading Conservatives had been demanding for months.

Americans of every political persuasion stood solidly behind the President and awaited the dramatic confrontation with Cuba's Russian masters. The result is history: Khrushchev retreated in the face of American determination and removed his missiles and bases.

Many Conservative leaders wish there were equally dramatic means of demonstrating the follies of Liberal domestic policies.

"Just as Mr. Kennedy got the whole people behind him on Cuba," wrote William Buckley, Jr., on November 18, 1962, "so a national leader, flourishing real photographs taken by our U-2s of money tippy-toeing out of the individual states into Washington, and creeping back after a long, lost weekend, vastly underweight—let those photographs be shown to the people before it is concluded that they have departed, forever, from conservatism."

Once they can dispel the smoke screen which surrounds our national march down the road to statism and away from individual initiative, Conservative spokesmen believe, Americans will unite solidly behind programs which will return our country to the philosophy which made it great.

The Conservative Revival, revealed as it is in continued Congressional defeats of Liberal welfare programs, will die a well-deserved death if Conservatives are to be content with stopping the opposition. Defeat of New Frontier legislation is not nearly enough.

Much as Conservatives may oppose Liberal legislative proposals, they must face up to the fact that these proposals have been spawned by real and pressing national problems. America's old folks are becoming more numerous with every passing year, and somehow they must pay for increasingly expensive medical care. Education, from kindergarten to graduate school, needs better financing. The problems of our cities are mounting as population shifts put more than 80 per cent of all Americans in metropolitan centers. And, despite our national affluence, our nation still has too much unemployment and want.

Do these national problems cry out for Medicare, federal aid to education, a new Department of Urban Affairs and new federally-financed welfare programs?

Of course not—not if Americans care about preserving individual responsibility and avoiding national bankruptcy. These Liberal programs have glitter and glamour, however, and they offer to the unwary an easy way out of our difficulties. They promise a softening of the jagged, hard realities of life, and they are merchandised in appealing packages by plausible-sounding salesmen.

They are, in short, offered to the electorate as easy solutions to very real problems. And even an obviously leaky life raft is likely to be grasped by a foundering swimmer in preference to a manual of instructions on water safety.

What, then, can Conservatives do to persuade their fellow Americans to reject gaudy Liberal philosophical merchandise and to accept a better Conservative product?

There is only one way, and that is to move to the offensive in today's Great Debate—to research, produce and sell better legislative programs than the Liberals have been promoting—to appeal to the common sense that guides the vast majority of Americans when they are given enough facts upon which to base a decision vitally affecting their future.

Conservatives have taken giant steps forward in recent years toward the formulation of attractive programs based on individual and community action. The Kerr-Mills Act, the Bow proposal, and new private insurance programs, all to be discussed in a later chapter, offer sound alternatives to Medicare. Recent legislative proposals for more realistic depreciation allowances and encouragement of plant investment would do more to relieve unemployment than any program for creating new federal jobs. Heightened local concern over the problems of education already is providing better schools and making federal aid to education more unnecessary than ever before. Conservative proposals for gradual reduction of farm controls and subsidies would bring sanity back to American agriculture more surely and less expensively than any Liberal theory yet expounded.

Conservatives *do* have better programs for the solution of our national problems *now*. But the public is not nearly so well informed about them as it is about Liberal approaches. As a result, the people are prone to believe that only the Liberals are striving for positive action.

How has the Conservative Revival been progressing since the dawn of this decade of the 1960s?

A barrage of Conservative writing—topped by Senator Barry Goldwater's surprise best seller, *The Conscience of a Conservative*—opened the new decade. There were mass meetings of anti-Communist groups, pleading for a stiffer stand against Red infiltrations and military advances around the world. And then there was that startling wave of Conservative sentiment sweeping the nation's college campuses, winning the minds of supposedly Liberal youth. A year later, M. Stanton Evans was to examine the collegiate phenomenon in his searching book, *Revolt on the Campus*.

July 1960 brought the spirited Conservative surge in the Republican National Convention at Chicago—a convention which had been carefully organized and disciplined to produce but one result, a show of complete unanimity for the foregone convention choice, Vice-President Nixon. Young Conservative Clubs sprang up as if by magic, shouting their support of their hero, Senator Goldwater. Telegrams poured in on the delegates from states in which no real Conservative strength was expected. For a brief moment, as the Goldwater boom reached its climax, the party pros were shaken. Then Goldwater, counting his strength and finding it insufficient to warrant a convention fight, stepped to the rostrum and asked that his name be withdrawn from consideration. Nixon won the nomination, but the Conservative wing of the party had demonstrated strength unknown since the death of Senator Robert Taft.

Two months later an enthusiastic throng at Sharon, Conn. founded the "Young Americans for Freedom," with a 12 point credo that declared:

We, as young Conservatives, believe:

1. In the individual's use of his free will.
2. Political freedom cannot exist without economic freedom.
3. The purpose of government is to protect freedom by preserving order, national defense, and the administration of justice.
4. When government ventures beyond those aims, it tends to diminish liberty.
5. The U. S. Constitution is the best document to empower government to fill its role and still restrain it from abuses of power.
6. The genius of the Constitution is in its reserving to the states the powers not specified for the federal government.
7. A free supply-and-demand system is most compatible with the requirements of personal freedom, constitutional government, and the maximum supplying of human needs.
8. Government should not interfere with the processes in (7) above.
9. National sovereignty must be maintained for national security.
10. International Communism is the greatest threat to our liberty.
11. The United States should stress victory over, not coexistence with, Communism.
12. That American foreign policy should be judged by the yardstick: Does it serve the just interests of the United States?

Within 18 months, the Young Americans for Freedom had snowballed into an organization capable of attracting 18,000 cheering young people to a March 1962 rally in New York's Madison Square Garden.

Meanwhile, the presidential campaign was being waged

with much sound and fury, but without either candidate being able to win much really enthusiastic support. Senator John Kennedy chose a moderately Liberal campaign course. Vice-President Nixon, unwilling to risk his chances on a real Conservative vs. Liberal showdown, pitched his appeal so close to Kennedy's on the political wavelength that voters were left with nothing but a choice between personalities. Kennedy's personal appeal was the greater. He squeezed into the White House in an election so amazingly close that the change of one vote in each precinct around the nation would have given Nixon the plurality.

Passing almost unnoticed in the popularity contest was the fact that generally Conservative Republican candidates captured 20 House of Representatives seats from the Democrats in the same election—an almost unprecedented feat for the losing party.

Conservatives cheered another election result in May 1961, when a little-known Goldwater Republican named John Tower scored an upset victory in the special election to fill the Senate seat vacated by Lyndon B. Johnson when he assumed the Vice-Presidency. The first Republican Senator elected by Texans since Reconstruction, Tower promptly made good on his campaign promises by speaking out loud and clear on the Senate floor for a variety of Conservative causes. He has been a leading Conservative spokesman ever since.

In other 1961 elections, Conservatives scored wins in many state and city campaigns, and improved their 1960 showing in several others.

In the traditionally Conservative South, voters voiced their dissatisfaction with the Liberal programs of the New Frontier by turning in increasing numbers to the Republican Party. The much-publicized "resignation rallies" in Texas brought life-long Democrats to public halls to announce their decisions to switch party affiliation. "At Fort Worth," reported *U.S. News and World Report,* in describing one meeting, "more than 700 people gathered in a ballroom. . . . Theme of the meeting: The Democratic Party nationally has gone far to the left, and deep-dyed 'conservatives' can expect little from Texas Democratic primaries and conventions." Long-dispirited Republican leaders in all the Southern states started making serious plans for 1962, and their efforts were evidenced in the important off-year election gains made by their party in the South.

On February 16, 1962, reported *National Review,* a letter was mailed to 50,000 New York State Conservatives announcing formation of the state Conservative Party. The new party is not expected to elect many candidates in the near future. But, *National Review* opined, if nothing else it will pull the New York Republican Party a little toward the right, just as the New York Liberal Party exerted a leftward pressure on the state Democratic Party.

All across the nation in the early 1960s there have been rumblings of dissatisfaction with continued deficit spending, with growing federal power at the expense of state authority, with foreign aid, with attempts to accommodate Russia, with our reluctance to take a firm stand against Fidel Castro and his Communist government in Cuba.

This dissatisfaction stirred radicals on the Far Right to organize in a dozen different extremist movements—the best known being the John Birch Society. By late 1962, membership in these extremist groups was estimated at more than 300,000, and their resources totalled at least $20 million.

Although they are ridiculed by Liberals and viewed with concern by more moderate Conservatives, the Right Wing groups represent still another evidence of the Conservative Revival. They are symptomatic of a growing concern that America has strayed too far from its traditional concepts of individual responsibility and constitutional limitation of federal power.

The great majority of Conservatives, apprehensive over the radical approaches advocated by the Far Right, believe that extremist accusations and hate-mongering can only hurt Conservative causes. Most Conservatives breathed a sigh of relief when voters repudiated Birchers and their sympathizers in the 1962 elections.

The pace of the Conservative Revival is reflected in the upsurge of Conservative expression in the nation's communications media. The Conservative message is coming through in books, magazines, television and radio.

Columnist Henry Hazlitt, writing in the October 12, 1959, issue of *Newsweek,* declared, "Although in practical politics, especially in America, the assumption of statism, socialism, paternalism, and inflation were never more prevalent, there are increasing signs in the academic and intellectual world of a turn in thought. More Conservative books have been written in 1959 than in any year of the last thirty."

Close on the heels of Hazlitt's column came Senator Goldwater's *The Conscience of a Conservative,* Alan Drury's *Advise and Consent,* Evans' *Revolt on the Campus,* Senator Tower's *A Program for Conservatives,* and several other Conservatively-oriented books, all of which commanded wide readership.

National Review's circulation has been climbing, and its publisher, William Buckley, Jr., now has a nationally-syndicated newspaper column, as does Senator Goldwater. Conservative television series and such radio programs as "Life Line" are attracting impressive audiences. The Conservative viewpoint is getting a better airing than ever before in the editorial columns and letters-to-the-editor sections of the nation's press.

Over the airways, on the printed page, and by word of mouth, the Conservative story is being told energetically and well. It will have to be told even more effectively, however, if it is to pull ahead of deeply entrenched Liberal philosophies in the years ahead.

The Conservative Revival in America had its beginnings in the months following the conclusion of World War II in 1945. It helped elect the 80th Congress which so frustrated President Truman's Liberal programs in 1947-48. It was a potent force in the landslide which swept in Dwight D. Eisenhower and his "Great Crusade" in 1952.

"One of the wonders of the postwar decade has been the revival of Conservatism in American politics and culture," Clinton Rossiter wrote in 1955. "After generations of exile from respectability, the word itself has been welcomed home with cheers by men who, a few short years ago, would sooner have been called arsonists than conservatives. ... We are behaving like men with something substantial to be conservative about. ... Not for 150 years have men who profess conser-

vative principles (or who hold them without professing them)
enjoyed so splendid an opportunity for political and intellectual leadership. . . ."

Conservatism still has a long way to go before it can
claim dominance in American political thought.

But there is no escaping the fact that a Conservative Revival is on.

III.

■ THIS WE BELIEVE

What is it all about, this idea of Conservatism?

What is there in this political way of life that a man can grab onto . . . trust . . . plot his course by?

Because Conservatism is old, and tested, and solid, it has been considered by some restless spirits to be drab. But true Conservatism is the essence of life. It is the grain of radium which has come down to us from the distillation of many tons of human trials and errors over countless centuries. Its great worth has only recently been rediscovered by many thousands of Americans who have recognized that *change* is not always *progress*.

No political idea is really new. Men had tried price controls and relief payments and production quotas long before the Roman Empire was founded. They had experimented with dictatorship, pure democracy, city states, aristocracy, monarchy, legislatures and a hundred other ideas of government long before Columbus sailed for the new world.

From all this experience have come certain beliefs about the nature of man and his government, and these form the foundation of Conservative principles.

Russell Kirk and Clinton Rossiter, two notable writers on Conservatism in modern America, have catalogued the principles which they have found to be most basic in Conservative thinking. Kirk lists 6 in *A Program for Conservatives*, and Rossiter includes 21 in *Conservatism in America*. Raymond Moley and William F. Buckley have made similar listings. Almost every Conservative spokesman from the 18th Century statesman Edmund Burke to the present has attempted to catalog the foundation stones of Conservative philosophy.

An even dozen basic Conservative principles may be sifted from these many declarations.

Conservatives believe in:

1. *The superiority of liberty over security.*

   Completely free men will not have guaranteed security, and completely secure men will not be free.

2. *The natural inequality of man—except in possession of a soul and an inviolable personality.*

   Men have vastly differing talents, ambitions, and intelligence. There is no way to level these differences with any lasting success, and attempts to level them will limit freedom.

3. *The principle that human nature is essentially unchanging.*

   In every man there is good and bad: generosity, selfishness, lust for power, compassion for the unfortunate, a desire to acquire possessions, a need for self-expression. Human nature has not changed essentially for many centuries, and it is not likely to change. Therefore, "government by law, not by men" is essential to the preservation of freedom.

4. *The necessity and inevitability of social and economic classes, and the need to keep the way clear for men to rise from one class to another.*

   The classless society is impossible in a world where men differ so widely in ability and ambition.

5. *The potential tyranny of unchecked majority rule.*

   Checks and balances must be established to protect minorities, and power should be diffused to prevent its concentration in any one group of citizens or any one branch of government.

6. *The rights of men as something earned—not given.*

   Freedom, opportunity, economic well-being—these are not easily won. They can be maintained only by constant effort.

7. *The esteem of private property rights as a foundation of liberty and progress.*

   The right of private ownership, and the right to enjoy the fruits of our labor, are among the most precious of human rights. True independence can never be enjoyed by one who must rely on other persons or agencies—especially government—for food, shelter, and material comforts.

8. *The importance of the lessons of history as a guide to the future.*

   The successes and failures of this nation and others in the past should be an indispensable reference in planning for tomorrow.

9. *The respect for inherited institutions and values.*

   Governmental principles and forms which have been tested and found to be sound should not be lightly discarded. Change is inevitable and desirable, but it should be orderly change, based on experience.

10. *The necessity of a free supply-and-demand economic system to guarantee both a maximum of personal freedom and the supplying of human needs.*

    When government attempts to control production, prices, demand, or other facets of the economy, imbalances occur which can only lead to further controls.

11. *The need for government to function with maximum thrift and efficiency, and within its financial means.*

    Expenditures should not exceed income, except when the security of the nation demands. Deficits incurred during periods of dire emergency should be made up as soon as possible.

12. *The placing of primary responsibility, wherever possible, in the individual, the community, and the state instead of in the federal government.*

    To insure the greatest possible responsiveness to the needs of the people, governmental activity should be performed by the smallest governmental unit capable of doing the job.

Each Conservative, individualist that he is, might compile a different list of principles, changing emphasis here, adding ideas there. Rossiter, for example, includes "the civilizing, disciplining, conserving mission of education" on his list, along with "the existence of immutable principles of universal justice," and others. The Young Americans for Freedom include an insistence that "national sovereignty must be maintained to guarantee our security."

John C. Calhoun paraphrased the principle of unchanging human nature in his declaration that "we must take men as they are, and do the best we can with them, constituted as they are." Benjamin Franklin stated the proposition of liberty over security by declaring that "those who would give up essential liberty to purchase a little temporary safety deserve neither liberty nor safety." And countless spokesmen for Conservatism have emphasized the idea that government must deal in the possible instead of the desirable—the real rather than the abstract—facts instead of wishes.

Are all these basic beliefs the sole property of Conservatives?

No.

Liberals, in general, recognize that men differ in talent and ambition. They take pride in American institutions and place value in the lessons of history. They love liberty.

In these areas, the differences between Conservatives and Liberals are in degree and emphasis. For example, although both espouse liberty, Liberals have consistently sought liberty for the masses in the maximum equality of all. Conservatives, as Gordon Harrison put it in *Road to the Right,* "have sought it (liberty) in guarantees of minority rights ... and in a 'natural order' which in theory assured the maximum social diversity." The respect for history and inherited institutions is less evident in the Liberal philosophy than in the Conservative. Liberals are prone to say "yes, but times have changed," forgetting the fact that the natural laws of economics and social relationships do not change.

Differences become more pronounced when it comes to majority rule, the laws of supply and demand, and government thrift. Liberals are much more willing to trust the shifting will of the majority. They put more faith in government planning of the economy than in the functioning of the free market. They place "what we need" above "what we can afford."

The conflict in ideas becomes most evident when the discussion turns to property rights, the necessity of earning the good things in life, and centralization of government.

Liberals traditionally have viewed property rights as being in conflict with human rights. They demand that all good things should be guaranteed to the inefficient and lazy as well as to the ambitious and the thrifty. And most of all, they insist that the federal government, through its huge resources and "overall view," can solve our problems more efficiently than can local or state governments.

Not so, answers Senator Strom Thurmond of South Carolina: "It is completely false to assume that the role of government must increase with growth in technology," he told the student body at Massachusetts Institute of Technology on April 28, 1961. "There is no necessity whatever for morality or political philosophy to change every time technology improves. The fundamental nature of men and their need to mix their labor with resources in order to produce consumer goods, their desire for sociability, their need for private property, are always the same, whatever the era of history. Jesus' teachings were not limited in their applicability to the ox-cart age, and neither were the Ten Commandments outmoded by the invention of the telephone."

Senator Goldwater sums up his ideas about the differences in basic philosophies with these words from *Conscience of a Conservative:*

"The root differences between the Conservatives and the Liberals of today," he wrote, "is that Conservatives take account of the whole man, while the Liberals tend to look only at the material side of man's nature. The Conservative believes that man is, in part, an economic, an animal creature; but that he is also a spiritual creature with spiritual needs and spiritual desires. What is more, these spiritual needs and desires reflect the *superior* side of man's nature, and thus take precedence over his economic wants.... Liberals, on the other hand—in the name of a concern for 'human beings'—regard the satisfaction of economic wants as the dominant mission of society. They are, moreover, in a hurry. So that their characteristic approach is to harness the society's political and economic forces into a collective effort to *compel 'progress.'* In this approach, I believe, they fight against nature."

This, then, is the idea of Conservatism.

It is the belief that Americans would rather be free to shoot for the moon—and risk failing—that be satisfied with mediocrity and a secure living, guaranteed and controlled at every step by a paternal federal government.

Conservatism is not attractive to those who are fearful of rough-and-tumble competition. While it offers more glorious rewards, both material and spiritual, it is booby-trapped with greater risks.

It is a matter of grave concern to Conservatives that so many modern Americans seem more willing to settle for security than to battle for opportunity. There was a time, and not so many decades ago, when Americans were so sure of their own abilities, and so confident of the essential rightness of limiting federal power, that the questions of 'planned economy' and 'cradle-to-grave welfare' were never seriously debated.

Can a generation grow from childhood to old age in the knowledge that the government will provide—and still retain its self-reliance?

Conservatives doubt it.

"But," cry the Liberals, "what about the weak, the aged, the sick, the victims of circumstance? You heartless Conservatives would let them starve in order to insure freedom for the strong!"

It is an old and repetitious argument, and one which Conservatives have allowed to take root.

The truth is that Conservatives are just as concerned as Liberals about the well-being of those who cannot support themselves. But Conservatives seek answers to the problem in the family, the church and synagogue, the private charitable organization, the community. Liberals insist that it is a problem only the federal government can solve. Somehow, they believe, it is better to send the dollars to Washington, pay a handling charge, and let them be distributed from there.

Conservatives are sure that this Liberal preoccupation with guaranteed security—a preoccupation that makes them willing to turn increasingly to the federal government—tends to weaken the daring and productivity which create more jobs and a higher standard of living for all.

"Nothing is more fatal than the present fashion among

intellectual leaders of extolling security at the expense of freedom," Peter Hayek wrote in *The Road to Serfdom*. "It is essential that we should re-learn frankly to face the fact that freedom can be had only at a price and that as individuals we must be prepared to make severe material sacrifices to preserve our liberty."

Herbert Hoover, in his long career of public service, often stressed the necessity of encouraging natural human ambitions in the creation of a climate for maximum productivity.

"And society, to be successful, must secure the effort and initiative of its citizens," he once declared. "Otherwise, it will stagnate or degenerate. To meet its needs and to advance its civilization, it must encourage the impulses which motivate the individual to action and achievement. Therefore, any workable philosophy of society or framework of government must take account of the raw materials of human nature, from which its motivations of human drives arise, if it would build for the betterment of the nation."

Do Conservatives believe that *all* functions of government can best be performed by the communities and the states?

Of course not.

One has only to imagine locally-managed military forces, post office service, foreign relations, space exploration programs—or a lack of centrally-directed air traffic control or tariff regulation—to picture the chaos which would result.

In the fiercely individualistic years following the Revolutionary War, we tried just such a decentralized system under the Articles of Confederation. It worked so inefficiently that the newly-liberated States soon banded together under the Constitution, which granted to the federal government such powers as those of providing national defense, maintaining internal order, administering justice, and removing obstacles to the free interchange of goods.

The framers of the Constitution recognized that a strong central government is necessary to maintain the freedoms for which the Revolution had been fought, and to establish institutions which could strengthen national unity. But they were careful to write in a provision that all powers not specifically delegated to the federal government were to be reserved to the states, and to the people. They went a step further, establishing such a tortuous amendment procedure that no momentary swell of majority sentiment could change the basic document of national government. In more than a century and a half, only 13 amendments have been approved, and two of those—Prohibition and Repeal—cancelled each other out.

Conservatives recognize the unifying values and the practical necessity of federal government. They know that it can maintain individual freedom by curbing the abuses of Big Business, Big Labor, or sectional interests.

But Conservatives insist that federal government be limited to those powers *granted by the Constitution*. They know that, if it is allowed to assume unlimited power, the government of even such a freedom-loving republic as ours can soon become restrictive and, finally, tyrannical.

Impatience with the sometimes cumbersome progress of government by free men under a self-imposed constitution has led many a nation to succumb to the gaudy lure of the "efficiencies" of the super-state.

Because Mussolini made the trains run on time, Italians in the 1920s were willing to surrender their hard-won freedoms to his government. They could hardly have imagined that by 1929 the Secretary-General of the Fascist Party, Signor Turati, would be saying: "We certainly are undemocratic if democracy means the conferring of powers on those above by those below. An army takes its orders, goes out and executes them, dies if necessary. But it does not question those orders, nor does it elect officers."

Freedom may be lost in many ways. One of the surest, Conservatives believe, is in the surrender—all at once, or gradually—of individual powers to a paternal national government.

What kind of person is the American Conservative of the '60s?

Liberals are fond of picturing him as rich, selfish, anti-

ntellectual. Actually, he is to be found at every economic,
ocial, and intellectual level.

"The people we call 'conservatives' are not restricted to
ny social class or any economic occupation, or any level
of formal education," says Kirk. "Some are physicians, and
ome engine drivers, and some professors, and some clerks,
nd some bankers, diemakers and soldiers. . . . Conservatism
nd Liberalism and Radicalism are states of mind, not of the
ocketbook. The United States throughout most of our his-
ory has been a nation substantially conservative, though
ich men have exerted less direct influence upon government
ere than almost anywhere else in the world. Conserva-
ism is something more than mere solicitude for tidy incomes."

Today's Conservative can be found in large numbers in
oth the great political parties. Some of the nation's most
horoughly Conservative political leaders are Southern Demo-
rats, and some of the most Liberal-minded are Eastern Re-
ublicans.

But it cannot be denied that the Republican Party, national-
y, has for the past century been the most Conservative of
he two. In a recent analysis of Senate voting, made by the
Americans for Constitutional Action, the five senators who
voted most conservatively were all Republicans (Democratic
Senator Byrd of Virginia was the sixth most conservative,
owever), and the five who voted the Liberal position most
onsistently were all Democrats. Senate Republicans, in general, voted as Conservatives well over half the time, the
tudy revealed, and most Democrats voted consistently as
Liberals.

Conservatism is not limited to any section of the nation,
either, although the South and the Midwest have been more
onsistently Conservative than most other geographical areas.

What is it Conservatives seek to conserve?

Benjamin Disraeli, the British Prime Minister, had a wonderful answer when questioned about it nearly a century ago:

"We are told that a working man cannot be conservative
because he has nothing to conserve—he has neither land nor
apital," replied Disraeli. "As if there were not other things
n the world as precious as land and capital!" The working
man, he added, has liberty, security of person and home,

equal protection of the laws, the right to the fruit of his industry. "Surely these are privileges worthy of being preserved! And if that be the case, is it so wonderful that the working classes are conservative?"

Today Americans have great traditions to conserve. It is on the foundation of those traditions that we can build a nation in which freedom, prosperity, and the riches of the spirit are within the reach of all.

IV.

■ THEY SPEAK FOR CONSERVATISM

When Russell Kirk wrote that Conservatives spring from every walk of life, from every intellectual strata, and from every economic level, he might well have been speaking in particular of the men who are spearheading the Conservative movement of the 1960s.

Senator Harry Byrd was a newspaper publisher and an apple grower before entering Virginia politics. Senator Byrd was nearly 40 when the youngest current Conservative giant, William Buckley, was born. Buckley, Yale-educated and polysyllabic, makes his living as an author, editor and lecturer. Senator Barry Goldwater of Arizona left college during his freshman year to work in his family's Phoenix department store.

Charles Halleck, Minority Leader of the U. S. House of Representatives, was a Phi Beta Kappa at the University of Indiana and first made his mark as an Indiana prosecuting attorney. Everett Dirksen of Illinois, Minority Leader of the U. S. Senate, managed a dredging company and served as Pekin, Illinois finance commissioner before going to Congress. John Tower of Texas stepped into the Senate from the faculty of Midwestern University. Author Raymond Moley became disillusioned with the New Deal after serving as an FDR Braintruster and has been campaigning for Conservatism ever since.

Some of the men in the forefront of today's Conservative movement are intellectuals, and some have had only passing acquaintanceship with formal education. Some are relatively wealthy, but many more face a continuing battle to make ends meet. A majority are Republicans, but many are Democrats. They come from the Midwest, the South, New England, the Southwest, the Far West.

They have one common bond: a deep faith in Conservative principles, and with it a determination to bring about a rebirth of those principles in the governing of the nation.

THE CONGRESSIONAL LEADERS

Sen. Barry Goldwater, R. Arizona

A tireless battler against the Welfare State and an outspoken advocate of individual freedom and responsibility, Barry Goldwater is the recognized leader of resurgent American Conservatism.

Born January 1, 1909, in Phoenix, he is the eldest of three children born to pioneer Arizona drygoods merchant Baron Goldwater and his wife Josephine, Arizona's first registered nurse. After a boisterous adolescence, more noted for achievement in athletics, photography and electronics than for academic excellence, Goldwater left the University of Arizona to work in the family department store in 1929. He and his brother Bob brought the business through the Depression to a position of eminence among American specialty stores for women. Then Barry left the presidency of Goldwater's, Inc. to become a World War II fighter pilot.

In 1949, he won a seat on the Phoenix City Council, and three years later he rode the Eisenhower tide to a surprising victory in a Senatorial campaign against Majority Leader Ernest W. McFarland.

Goldwater made his first Senate speech in opposition to federal economic controls, and he has been blasting away at federal domination of individuals and the states ever since.

A man of many talents, he is a jet pilot and a major general in the Air Force Reserve, a renowned photographer, author of the best-selling *Conscience of a Conservative* and other books, and one of the most sought-after speakers in America.

Blessed with energy and charm, Goldwater has won millions of friends, both for himself and for his uncompromising Conservative principles.

Rep. Charles A. Halleck, R. Indiana

"I am a gut fighter," Charles Halleck has often declared in assessing his performance as House Minority Leader.

It requires the courage and tenacity of a "gut fighter" to lead the coalition of Republicans and Conservative Democrats in holding the line against the Liberal majority in today's House of Representatives.

Halleck exhibits amazing political skill in maneuvering his outnumbered forces in their fight for fiscal sanity and against the march toward statism.

Born August 22, 1900, at DeMotte, Indiana, he was a *cum laude* graduate of Indiana University in 1922 and was elected to Phi Beta Kappa. He earned his law degree at IU in 1924, and that same year was elected prosecuting attorney of Jasper and Newton Counties. In 1934, he won a special Congressional election and has served in the House from that time to the present. He was elected House Majority Leader of the 80th and 83rd Congresses, and succeeded Joe Martin as Minority Leader at the start of the 86th.

Once an ardent isolationist, Halleck was convinced of the need for American leadership in world affairs during World War II and has worked in the intervening years to assure that leadership.

A veteran of World War I, Halleck is a member of the American Legion and a battler for a militarily strong America. He is an avid hunter and fisherman, and enjoys golf.

But Halleck, who works at top speed from dawn to late at night, has little time for anything but his immensely responsible job.

Sen. Everett M. Dirksen, R. Illinois

Everett Dirksen, snow-thatched master of melodious oratory and Minority Leader of the United States Senate, went from business to municipal finance to Congress during the 15 years following World War I.

Born in Pekin, Illinois, a town which he still calls home, on January 4, 1896, Dirksen attended the University of Minnesota and then served with the Army in World War I, first as a private and later as a second lieutenant.

He became manager of the Cook Dredging Company in 1922. His first venture into public service came in 1927, when he accepted the post of Commissioner of Finance in his native Pekin.

Dirksen was elected to the U. S. House of Representatives from the 16th Illinois District in 1933 and served there from the 73rd through the 80th Congresses. In 1949 he moved up to the Senate, where he has remained despite determined Liberal opposition.

A master of political craftsmanship, Dirksen has learned how to make the most effective use of available voting power to battle for Conservative programs.

Sen. John G. Tower, R. Texas

Few Americans outside Texas had heard of tiny John Tower before 1961. But today he stands among the leaders in the battle for Conservative principles.

Tower gained his Senate seat in a special election to fill the vacancy caused by the election of Lyndon Johnson to the Vice-Presidency. In scoring his upset victory, Tower became the first Republican elected to the Senate from Texas since Reconstruction days.

Born in Houston on September 29, 1925, Tower is the son of a Methodist minister. After serving three years aboard a Navy gunboat in World War II, he resumed his college career and earned his B.A. degree in polical science from Southwestern University, Georgetown, Texas, in 1948. In 1951, he joined the political science faculty at Midwestern University, Wichita Falls, Texas, and taught there until June, 1960. He won his M.A. degree in 1953 from Southern Methodist University.

"I am opposed to the New Frontier—its farm program, federal aid to education, medical care to the aged, higher taxes, foreign aid, and wasteful domestic spending," he declared in a *Time* interview published June 9, 1961.

The energetic young senator has backed up his words with his voting record ever since assuming his Senate seat.

A member of the Senate Banking and Currency Committee and the Labor and Public Welfare Committee, Tower advocates positive Conservative programs and was one of six senators named to a joint Senate-House committee to draft a statement of Republican principles in 1962.

Sen. Harry F. Byrd, D. Virginia

Long regarded as Capitol Hill's most persuasive advocate of sound fiscal policy and the leader of Democratic Conservatism, Harry Byrd is revered by members of both major parties.

Born June 10, 1887, at Martinsburg, West Virginia, he achieved a measure of prominence at the age of 15, when he acquired a bankrupt Virginia newspaper and put it on a paying basis. A few years later he entered the business of apple growing. Today he publishes two Virginia daily newspapers, the *Winchester Star* and the *Harrisonburg News-Record*, and he is listed by the Department of Agriculture as the largest individual apple grower in the world.

Senator Byrd attended Shenandoah Valley Academy. He made his first venture into politics before he was 21, winning a seat on the Winchester City Council, and was elected to the Virginia Senate at 27.

After serving a term as Governor of Virginia, he was appointed to fill out the unexpired U.S. Senate term of Claude Swanson in 1933. He has served since that year without interruption.

His Senate committee assignments reflect his interest in government economy. He has been chairman of the Select Committee on Government Reorganization and the Joint Committee on Reduction of Non-essential Federal Expenditures. He became chairman of the Finance Committee in 1955.

His advocacy of free enterprise solutions, and his insistence on pay-as-you-go financing, have guided his staunchly Conservative voting through all his years in the Senate.

Rep. Donald C. Bruce, R. Indiana.

Traditionally Conservative Indiana sent Donald Bruce to the House of Representatives from its 11th District in 1960. In the brief time since his election, he has gained national recognition as a powerful voice for Conservatism.

Born at Troutsville, Pa., on April 27, 1921, he attended Allentown, Pa., High School and Muskingum College, Ohio. He was an Indiana radio station program director and general manager for many years before entering politics. Bruce now makes his home in Indianapolis.

An advocate of individual responsibility and strong local government, Bruce has been an effective foe of federal government expansion since coming to Congress.

"If you're looking for something for nothing, don't vote for me," he told voters during his 1960 campaign. "My only pledge is to work to uphold the Constitution of the United States—to preserve an environment, economic and social, wherein every individual man may attempt to fulfill his desires and dreams."

Sen. Karl E. Mundt, R. South Dakota

Perhaps the best known of the solid Midwest Conservatives is Karl Mundt. A tireless warrior against Communist infiltration, he was co-author with Richard Nixon of the famed Mundt-Nixon Anti-Communist Bill, and was acting chairman of the House Un-American Activities Committee during the espionage hearings which resulted in the conviction of Alger Hiss.

Mundt was born June 3, 1900, at Humboldt, South Dakota, earned his bachelor's degree from Carleton College, Northfield, Minn., and his master's degree from Columbia University. After teaching speech in high school and college, and serving as a school superintendent, Mundt tried his hand for a time at insurance and investments.

He won a House of Representatives seat in the First South Dakota District in 1938, and his Senate tenure dates from 1949.

Mundt authored the bill creating the Voice of America, and his resolution in favor of the United Nations Educational, Scientific and Cultural Organization led to the creation of that U. N. agency.

He is co-author of the Mundt-Coudert Amendment to reform the Electoral College system of electing the President and Vice-President.

A man of many interests, Mundt is an outdoor sportsman

and conservationist, an organizer of the National Forensic League, a former vice-president of the South Dakota Poetry Association, and a former Kiwanis district governor.

Sen. Strom Thurmond, D. South Carolina

Lieutenant Colonel Strom Thurmond sailed into Normandy by glider on D-Day, 1944, and stayed to win the Bronze Star, the Purple Heart and a chestful of other decorations. Today he is a major general in the Army Reserve.

The courage he displayed in combat has cropped up time and again in his political career. He delights in throwing himself headlong into controversy, leading the fight against "muzzling" the military, arguing the merits of racial segregation, battling for state's rights. Opposition from his own party, or from Conservatives north of the Mason-Dixon Line, does not awe him.

Strom Thurmond was born December 5, 1902, at Edgefield, S. C. He was graduated from Clemson College in 1923, taught agriculture in high school, and then studied law at night to gain admittance to the South Carolina Bar in 1930. He served as a circuit judge, state senator, and governor of South Carolina before his successful campaign as a write-in candidate for U.S. Senator in 1954.

In 1948, he was a candidate for President on the States' Rights Party ticket and amassed 1,169,073 votes.

Thurmond keeps a set of barbells in his office and works out daily in the Senate gym. He needs to be in top physical condition to fight his continuing battles for Southern Conservatism.

Rep. Melvin R. Laird, R. Wisconsin.

Melvin Laird was a boy wonder of 24 when he was elected to the Wisconsin State Senate in 1946. Laird had just returned from Navy service in the Pacific Theater, where he was wounded in action. His keen mind and astute political sense soon rocketed him to prominence in Wisconsin government.

In 1952 he waged a successful campaign for election to the U. S. House of Representatives from Wisconsin's Seventh District. He is now serving his sixth term in office, and has been a fighter for Conservative principles ever since going to Washington. He has served on the House Appropriations Committee since 1953.

Born September 1, 1922, he earned a Bachelor of Arts degree at Carleton College. Rep. Laird is married, the father of three children, and has been active in the American Legion, the Veterans of Foreign Wars, Disabled American Veterans, and Military Order of the Purple Heart.

Rep. Peter Frelinghuysen, Jr., R. New Jersey

Peter Frelinghuysen has degrees from both Princeton (B.A.) and Yale (LL.B.), the latter earned in 1941. Shortly after winning his law degree, he was called to World War II service with the Navy. After the war, Frelinghuysen served on the Foreign Affairs Task Force of the Hoover Commission and then became a director of the Trust Company of Morris County, New Jersey.

He was elected to the U. S. House of Representatives from New Jersey's Fifth District in 1952, at the age of 36. For more than a decade he has been one of the most articulate advocates of Conservative programs.

Rep. Frelinghuysen is married and the father of five children.

THE WRITERS AND THE SPEAKERS

Raymond Moley

Chosen to serve as one of Franklin Delano Roosevelt's original Brain Trusters, Dr. Moley soon became apprehensive about the New Deal's tendency toward statism. He has been writing and speaking against the concentration of power in Washington since the mid-1930s.

An Ohioan, he was born in Berea on September 27, 1886, and won his Ph.B. from Baldwin-Wallace College. He took his A.M. degree at Oberlin, and his Ph.D. at Columbia University.

A teacher, school superintendent, and college professor in the 1920's, he became Assistant Secretary of State under Roosevelt in 1933. His disillusionment with the New Deal was mirrored in his book *After Seven Years,* published in 1939. In 1952, he wrote *How To Keep Our Liberty,* and he has many other conservatively-oriented books to his credit.

He is best known today as a featured columnist in *Newsweek* magazine, and as a lecturer. Dr. Moley makes his home in New York City.

William F. Buckley

Leader of the current Conservative youth movement (he was born in 1925) is William Buckley. Son of a businessman who made millions in Latin-American oil, Buckley was a Conservative firebrand in his undergraduate days at Yale.

In 1951, his best-selling *God and Man at Yale* blasted that university's faculty for teaching "anti-capitalist and anti-Christian" philosophies. It rocketed Buckley to national prominence and embroiled him in the never-ending controversy on which he thrives.

He later co-authored *McCarthy and His Enemies,* a defense of the fiery Wisconsin senator, and more recently has written *Up from Liberalism,* a scathing denunciation of Liberal views. In 1962 he began writing a nationally-syndicated newspaper column, "A Conservative View."

In *National Review,* Buckley battles Communism, the Welfare State, the graduated income tax, and Liberals in and out of government.

Although his awesome vocabulary and intellectual approach make rapport with the common man difficult, Buckley has won widespread admiration from Conservatives for his outspoken attacks on Liberal positions.

Fulton Lewis, Jr.

Fulton Lewis was born in Washington, D.C., in 1903 and never has strayed for long from the nation's capital.

After attending the University of Virginia, he was a reporter and city editor of the *Washington Herald,* and later was syndicated by International News Service.

Since 1937, he has been a national affairs commentator for the Mutual Broadcasting Company, except for a brief stint as a war correspondent in 1945. He has written a widely-read column for King Features.

Lewis, who has been fighting federal government centralization for many years and exposing the dangers of radi-

cal Liberalism, was founder and first president of the Radio
Correspondents Association.

His daily radio news analysis is heard all over the nation,
and he is in great demand as a lecturer.

Holmes Alexander

Through his nationally-syndicated newspaper columns,
Holmes Alexander has become one of the nation's best-known
Conservative spokesmen.

A West Virginian, born at Parkersburg in 1906, Alexander
was graduated from Princeton University and then studied at
Cambridge University in England. He served four years in
the Maryland General Assembly (1931-35) and has been
a columnist on national affairs since 1947.

Among his many books are biographical studies of Aaron
Burr and Martin Van Buren. He served as an Air Force major in World War II.

Alexander now makes his home in Baltimore.

David Lawrence

A Washington correspondent for more than half a century,
David Lawrence has been influencing public opinion through
magazines, books and newspapers since the administration
of President Taft.

Born on Christmas Day, 1888, in Philadelphia, he
earned his B.A. degree at Princeton in 1910 and launched
his reporting career with the Associated Press in Washington
that same year. He became a Washington correspondent for
the *New York Evening Post* in 1916 and later wrote for news
services and magazines in the Capitol City.

In 1948 he became president and editor of *U.S. News and
World Report,* and his magazine has been gaining in stature
and influence ever since. His syndicated newspaper column
is read throughout the nation, and he has written seven
books on politics and government.

Although death stilled his persuasive voice in 1953, the
legacy of Senator Robert A. Taft of Ohio is still much in
evidence in the Conservatism of the 1960s. Taft, one of several outstanding Conservatives elected to Congress in 1938,

led the fight against the rising tide of Liberalism for more than a decade. At times it seemed he was standing almost alone. Recognized by both friends and foes alike as one of the most effective men ever to serve in the Senate, he led the Conservative cause through its grimmest days.

Senator Styles Bridges of New Hampshire, who died in 1961, was another Conservative giant. A teacher, editor, and farm bureau secretary before coming to the Senate in 1937, he served his nation with energy, intellect, and integrity for nearly a quarter century.

There have been many others who contributed to the present regeneration of Conservatism. Former President Herbert Hoover, who survived the defamation of Liberals to become an honored elder statesman, has written and spoken on behalf of Conservative principles with telling effect.

Former President Dwight D. Eisenhower and Vice-President Richard Nixon, although regarded more as middle-ground Republicans than Conservatives, did much for the Conservative cause by applying the brakes to rampant Liberalism as practiced under the New Deal and Fair Deal.

Authors Russell Kirk, Clinton Rossiter, Peter Hayek, Gordon Harrison and many others have made their marks. Columnists, commentators, businessmen, film actors, and members of a dozen other professions have contributed to the rebirth of the Conservative idea.

New spokesmen are rising every year, both in and out of government.

Their voices will be heard.

2.

The Deep and Durable Roots

V.

■ OUR CONSERVATIVE REVOLUTIONARIES

Revolution!

The very name has a wild, lawless ring to it.

It calls to mind scenes of vengeful violence—bloodthirsty French peasants cheering at each swish of the guillotine—bomb-hurling Bolsheviks blasting their way into a tragic new era of Russian history—Castro's bearded firing squads exterminating their Cuban opposition.

Almost every revolution has brought—along with the overthrow of existing government—confiscation of property, suspension of democratic processes, replacement of old tyrants with new.

Not so with the American Revolution of 1776.

The American colonists were, for the most part, Englishmen who had grown up with English law and English representative government. They wanted no radical changes in governmental form. They were simply fed up with the abuses heaped upon them by that incredibly stupid tyrant, George II, and wanted to regain the freedom they had enjoyed under earlier monarchs.

John Adams expressed the general feeling when he wrote in 1775, "The patriots of this province desire nothing new; they wish only to keep their old privileges. They were, for 50 years, allowed to tax themselves, and govern their internal concerns as they thought best. Parliament governed their trade as they thought fit. This plan they wish may continue forever."

How long and hard the colonists tried to work out a peaceful settlement of their grievances with the mother country is sometimes obscured by the excitement of the Boston Tea Party and the deathless oratory of Patrick Henry.

But try they did, for these fathers of today's America were,

57

for the most part, Conservatives. They mistrusted radical change—and violent change in particular. They would have continued as loyal British subjects for many a year had they been able to retain their freedom, and had King and Parliament not persisted in looking on them as naughty children who were insufferably demanding about having a hand in their own taxing and governing.

Faced with choosing between secure order and dangerous freedom, however, these colonial Conservatives cast their lot with freedom.

American Conservatives have been making the same choice ever since.

What sort of men were these who affixed their names so boldly to the Declaration of Independence, knowing full well that if the Revolution failed they stood to lose not only their property but their liberty and perhaps their lives as well? What manner of Americans were these who first tried out a loose confederation of sovereign states and then drafted a Constitution bolstered from beginning to end with every conceivable safeguard against federal tyranny over individuals and states?

First of all, they were dedicated to the ideal of liberty—not only liberty of a young nation from the whims of a tyrannical monarch, but liberty of individuals to develop their God-given talents to the full and to enjoy the products of their labor.

They were men who believed, as the Virginia Declaration of Rights of 1776 declared, "That no free government, or the blessings of liberty, can be preserved to any people but by a firm adherence to justice, moderation, temperance, frugality and virtue, and by a frequent recurrence to fundamental principles."

The men who founded the American republic and guided it through its perilous early years were for the most part men of property and influence. Yet they were determined that there should be no privileged aristocracy on this side of the Atlantic—no barriers to keep free men from rising as high as their talents and energies would carry them.

They were just as determined that the shifting sentiments of the majority should not keep government policy dancing about like a leaf in the wind. They provided that the Senate should be elected by the state legislatures; that the actual selection of the President should be made by an electoral college; and, finally, that a non-elective Supreme Court should stand guard over the government machinery.

No one was more aware than John Adams that danger lurks in any system of unchecked majority rule. "The fundamental article of my political creed," he wrote, "is that despotism, or unlimited sovereignty, or absolute power, is the same in a majority of a popular assembly, an aristocratical council, an oligarchical junto, and a single emperor. . . ."

Cautious as these Conservative statesmen were in their establishment of Constitutional checks and balances, in their reserving to the states and the people of all powers not specifically delegated to the federal government, they met bitter opposition from a sizeable segment of the American public which was against even that much centralized federal control.

Only the reassurances of their revered military leader, George Washington, and the brilliant arguments set forth by Alexander Hamilton, James Madison and John Jay in *The Federalist,* turned the tide in favor of ratification of the Constitution.

The Americans who launched a new nation in 1789 were determined to maintain home rule, and to keep the national government within its Constitutional bounds.

THE FEDERALISTS

George Washington was first in war, first in peace, first in the hearts of his countrymen, and the first great Conservative leader of the new American republic.

He was the unquestioned leader of the Federalists, whose goal of "a more perfect union" had led to the abandonment of the unworkable Articles of Confederation and the adoption of the Constitution. Washington had rallied the ragged, exhausted Continental armies and led them to victory over the world's greatest military power; he had served with distinction as president of the Constitutional Convention; and he had been a leader in the successful campaign for Constitutional

ratification. The new nation held him in such high regard
that he was unanimously elected the first President of the
United States of America.

Washington's primary task in his eight years as Chief Executive was to build from the noble blueprint of the Constitution a governmental structure that would serve the needs
of a struggling young nation without taking from its people
the liberties so recently won on the battlefields of the Revolution.

It was not an easy task.

Each of the 13 original states was determined to maintain
as much local sovereignty as possible. The stirring industrialism of the North put its interests in direct conflict with those
of the agricultural South. And a citizenry still exulting over
its emancipation from the taxation and tyranny of the British
Crown was far from willing to submit to new taxation and
new controls by a strong central government.

But, firmly and patiently, and using the full weight of his
enormous prestige, Washington rode out the storms of sectionalism and resistance to federal authority which might have
sunk the fragile new American ship of state had a lesser
pilot been at the helm. Remaining aloof from partisan conflicts, he was able to mold the philosophies of the Constitution into practical, workable governmental action and to
orient it in such a conservative direction that not even the
popular pressures exerted by Jefferson and Jackson could
appreciably change the course.

As his retirement to Mount Vernon drew near, Washington
prepared his final message to the nation he had served so
well. It was a collection of admonitions for the future—a bit
of fatherly advice from a wise old man who was uneasy
about trends he saw taking shape in America.

Known as his Farewell Address, it warned against sectional rivalries, foreign entanglements, the divisive effects of
political parties, the endangering of the public credit, and the
piling up of a federal debt we might some day be unable to
pay off.

We read the Farewell Address today with some apprehension. How could Washington have looked into the future with

such clarity? And how could we have managed to disregard his advice so completely?

Second only to Washington among the Federalists—the Conservative statesmen who launched the American republic in the final 13 years of the Eighteenth Century—was Alexander Hamilton.

Hamilton first attracted Washington's attention for his brilliant service as an officer in the Revolution. An energetic, tough-minded and articulate man, Hamilton moved to the forefront of American political leaders in the postwar era. His labors on behalf of Constitutional ratification and his knowledge of public finance made him the logical choice for Secretary of the Treasury in Washington's cabinet.

In his new post he rapidly established himself as the second most powerful man in the government. Systematic, efficient, tireless and dictatorial, he swept aside all opposition in his one-man crusade to put the new nation on a firm financial footing. He demanded that the federal government fund the national debt, assume the state debts, and establish a national bank. He battled for high tariffs to protect the blossoming young American industries. Only by taking these steps, he declared, could the United States be sure of independence and progress at home, and respect abroad.

Hamilton's insistence that America's only hope lay in a strong central government embroiled him in a bitter ideological duel with Thomas Jefferson and put him at odds with many of his more moderate fellow Federalists. Many of his views are not accepted by Conservatives today.

But it was in large part due to Hamilton's efforts that America, on the eve of the Nineteenth Century, was more than a loosely organized collection of jealously bickering states. Because of him the nation was ready to enter its great century of westward expansion and industrial growth as a united, financially sound, efficiently governed nation.

America was blessed with many great statesmen in the era of Federalism. James Madison, whose massive contributions to the writing of the Constitution won him the title of "father" of that document, and whose thoughtful logic in *The Federalist* helped secure its ratification, must be placed high on any listing of national founders. John Adams, who battled for limitations of the powers of federal government and the principle of checks and balances in the Constitution, and who succeeded Washington in the Presidency, is another.

The Federalists believed that all men, even the best, were ruled primarily by their passions. "The aim of government, they declared, was not to try to escape the influence of passions, but to manage them—not to make men reasonable, but to use their unreason," wrote Gordon Harrison in *Road to the Right*.

They understood human nature—its capacity for greatness and its capacity for evil—and they established a government which has harnessed the energies of that nature more efficiently than any other government in the long history of man.

It was in the clash between Secretary of the Treasury Hamilton and Secretary of State Jefferson that America's two great political parties had their philosophical foundations.

Hamilton advocated sound money, a national bank, firm foundations of national credit; Jefferson opposed the national bank, and saw in Hamilton's fiscal policies an attempt by the federal government to limit the sovereignty of the individual states. Hamilton dreamed of an industrialized America and was determined to protect the growth of business and industry with tariffs; Jefferson saw America's future in agriculture, and feared the moral and social effects of industrialization. Hamilton put his trust in strong central government, guided by Constitutional checks and balances; Jefferson wanted the real power left with the states, and was not convinced that the Constitution could adequately protect our liberties.

Modern Conservatives lean toward Hamilton's philosophy, except, perhaps, in his insistence on strong central government.

But even here the Hamiltonian theory is not as far from modern Conservatism as it might appear. It must be remembered that America, at the time of the Constitutional Convention, was almost completely decentralized. The nation was virtually defenseless. Differing laws, customs charges and currencies from state to state made it next to impossible to conduct interstate commerce. And the total lack of centralization in

uthority actually hindered the maintenance of order, justice
nd freedom.

What Hamilton and the other Federalists wanted was enough
entralized control to create from this uncoordinated collec-
on of petty sovereignties a truly unified nation.

It would be hard to imagine Hamilton—or Jefferson—sid-
ng with today's advocates of massive federal control over
he lives and property of American citizens.

Once their mission of establishing the new United States
overnment on a firm, conservative base was completed, the
Federalists began a rapid exit from the stage of American
istory. It was almost as if Federalism had been created for
hat one vital task, and none other.

The very austerity and aristocratic strength which made
Federalist leaders so uniquely qualified for the mission of
velding together the diverse interests of America into a unit-
d nation soon made them unacceptable to a citizenry
vhich worshipped the buckskinned frontiersman and the un-
ophisticated farmer and craftsman.

For a time the threat of the spread of radical French rev-
lutionary ideology helped keep Federalism alive. Disciples
of ultraliberalism so inflamed large segments of the American
opulation that the conservative principles of the Constitution
nd the new government itself were threatened in the late
790s.

Fear of subversion and even of counterrevolution so fright-
ned the administration of John Adams that it went to hysteri-
al extremes in forcing through the Alien and Sedition Acts
—designed not only to sift out foreign poisons, but to muzzle
he increasingly vocal Jeffersonian Republicans.

The Federalists went too far.

Their prosecutions under the Alien and Sedition Acts cre-
ted martyrs, and their "emergency" curbs on American lib-
rties caused a violent anti-Federalist reaction among those
vho valued freedom above all else.

At about the same time, the Federalists suffered a death
low in the retirement of Washington, Hamilton and other
key leaders. Federalism, it has been said, resigned before it
vas fired.

In 1800, the followers of Jefferson dealt the Federalist one of the worst beatings ever administered an American political party. Although the party was to linger on, bemoaning the bad new days, for some 16 more years, it never again was a real force on the American scene.

But Americans of every later era have owed the Federalist a huge debt for the legacy of the Constitution, the hammering out of a workable national government, the principl of financial stability and thrift, and the safe-guarding of national policy from the passions of shifting majorities.

America could not have asked for a firmer foundation.

VI.

■ JEFFERSONIANS, WHIGS AND REPUBLICANS

Vice-President Aaron Burr peered through the early morning mists shrouding Weehawken Heights, took hasty aim and fired.

Alexander Hamilton fell mortally wounded, victim of the most famous duel ever fought on American soil.

The year was 1804, and Hamilton's Federalist Party already had been dealt its mortal blow in the victory of Thomas Jefferson's Democratic Republicans four years earlier. Now Burr's dueling pistol had stilled Federalism's most persuasive voice.

America had moved into a new era of democratic feeling —one which was to extend voting rights, subject more public officials to direct election, provide greater public educational facilities, and destroy Hamilton's cherished National Bank. The Jeffersonians and the later Jacksonians were determined to tear down the nationalistic, aristocratic government structures erected by the Federalists. They succeeded in inflicting major damage, but the foundations remained firm for generations after their assault.

The man who did most to retain Federalist ideals in American government—and to add some Conservative principles of his own—was John Marshall.

John Adams appointed Marshall Chief Justice of the Supreme Court in the dying days of his administration, and the Virginian was destined to serve as a counterbalance to unchecked democracy until late in the second term of Andrew Jackson.

Marshall established the Supreme Court as the final word in American justice. He extended its authority over all the state courts, waged relentless war against the invasion of private property rights by state legislatures, and—most important—

made the Supreme Court the final judge of the Constitutionality of actions taken by Congress and the President.

So long as strong man Marshall was running the Supreme Court, the Constitution was securely entrenched as the bible of American government. Moreover, it was the Supreme Court which would decide how the Constitution was to be interpreted.

Marshall first established the principle of judicial review in the case of *Marbury v. Madison* in 1803. Here he stood up boldly against the Jeffersonians, reprimanded them, and made it stick. Despite howls of rage against the impertinence of the Court, Marshall went on to implant the principle of judicial review so firmly in the American government that it has never been dislodged.

It was a unique American contribution to the idea of government. And, although judicial review has at times thwarted the desires of the majority of Americans, it has time and again served as a steadying influence, keeping the course of the nation firmly steered in the direction pointed by the Constitution.

The Supreme Court is a traditionally Conservative institution, and not only because the age and legal backgrounds of the justices have tended to make them Conservative. The very presence of the Court, standing guard over the actions of popularly-elected legislators and the Executive, is a powerful deterrent to half-baked ideas and impulsive action.

It does not necessarily follow that Conservatives should never disagree with the actions of the Court. But they should defend its authority and its independence against all foes—or resign themselves to witnessing still another Constitutional bulwark of freedom weakened.

John Marshall's Court did much more than establish the right of judicial review. In *Dartmouth College v. Woodward*, it helped lay the groundwork for American industrial growth by ruling that a state does not have the right to alter the terms of a charter of incorporation. The decision gave the nation's rising industrialism a significant boost, since it gave corporations virtual immunity from political control.

In another 1819 decision, *McCulloch v. Maryland*, the Court echoed a Hamiltonian view, that of expansion of federal owers through the doctrine of implied powers. In this case, it was the right of the national government to charter the Bank of the United States that was upheld. In *Gibbons v. Ogden*, the Court again favored federal power in ruling that an act of Congress (regulating interstate commerce) must be held superior to any contradictory regulation issued by a state.

So it was, in case after case, that the Marshall Court challenged the Jeffersonian principles of state sovereignty and strict Constitutional interpretation.

Thomas Jefferson of Virginia was one of the true giants of American government. A lifelong advocate of the simple, honest ways of rural life in early America, he was at the same time an intellectual, a propertied aristocrat, and a shrewd practical politician.

Although his championing of more universal suffrage, his dislike of Hamilton's fiscal policies, and his distrust of federal power stamped him as a liberal in his day, he is revered by Conservatives of both parties today as an ideological ancestor.

The squire of Monticello trusted the wisdom of the common man, but he believed a man should own a small amount of property to qualify as a voter. He trusted individual action above collective action. He was a strict Constitutional constructionist, but he was flexible enough to buy the huge Louisiana Territory for what he considered a bargain price.

Most significant was his view on the individual differences of men. In a letter to John Adams, with whom he conducted a voluminous correspondence in his later years, Jefferson wrote:

"I will have to agree with you that there is a natural aristocracy among men. The grounds of this are virtue and talents. . . . There is also an artificial aristocracy, founded on wealth and birth, without either virtue or talents; for with these it would belong to the first class. The natural aristocracy I consider the most precious gift of nature, for the instruction, the trusts, and government of society. . . . The artificial aristocracy is a mischievous ingredient in govern ment, and provision should be made to prevent its ascen dancy."

Few modern Conservatives will argue with Jefferson there

The political heirs of Jefferson, almost without opposition maintained control of the federal government for 16 years aft er he had left the White House. James Madison, who broke with Hamilton over fiscal policy and centralized government and who favored France in her squabbles with England succeeded Jefferson to the Presidency in 1809. The War of 1812 roused sectional passions to such an extent that New Englanders (in the Hartford Convention of 1814) threatened to secede from the Union before they would obey Madison's call to furnish state troops to fight England.

But Madison had little trouble in maintaining national po litical control. James Monroe, who started his eight-year White House tenancy in 1817, had so little opposition that only one electoral vote was cast against him in 1820.

There was a shift to the right in 1824, when John Quincy Adams was elected. Adams, son of the last Federalist Presi dent, did not receive as many electoral votes as did Andrew Jackson. But the supporters of Henry Clay threw their votes to him when the House of Representatives was called upon to settle the issue, and that was enough to elect Adams.

Jackson was not to be denied, however. The angular old frontier war hero, supported with noisy fervor by the boom ing West, swept to victory in 1828, the first President to be elected by the modern Democratic Party.

From the day of Jackson's inauguration, when celebrating frontiersmen tracked mud onto the White House carpets, the eight-year rule of the "common man" was on. Jackson carried the swing away from Federalism the full 180 degrees. No President has ever been more hated and feared by men of property, position and aristocratic leanings. John Quincy Adams contemptuously called Jackson "a barbarian who could not write a sentence of grammar and hardly could spell his own name."

Jackson's aims were to extend suffrage still more widely,

o promote the popular election of more officials, to make
more federal jobs available for distribution by the party in
power—in short, to assure the rule of the majority.

But even this unpolished radical had his Conservative leanings. Few Americans have been more devoted to the cause
of individual freedom and opportunity. And few Presidents
have been more insistent on government economy. Incredible
as it seems in this day, Jackson was able not only to balance
the federal budget, but to retire completely the national debt!

RISE OF THE WHIGS

In 1834, Henry Clay was at last able to rally a coalition
of anti-Jackson forces. The man who "would rather be right
than President" had lost in two previous bids for the White
House—the most recent defeat being a bitter loss to Jackson
—and he was determined to beat the hated Democrats.

His coalition was a strange hodgepodge of National Republicans, Southern state's righters, and Democratic supporters
of the national bank. They had little to hold them together
but a common dislike of Jackson, however, and their ascendancy was to be not only brief but undistinguished.

They were aided by a rightward swing of the pendulum
of national feeling—a feeling expressed in the 1836 election
of the aristocratic New York Democrat, Martin Van Buren,
to succeed Jackson in the Presidency.

By 1840 the Whigs were strong enough to win. To be
sure of victory, they passed up such distinguished statesmen
as Clay and Daniel Webster in favor of the popular Indian
fighter, Gen. William Henry Harrison, hero of Tippecanoe.
The first Whig President was old and ailing, however, and
died within a month after taking office. His death brought
John Tyler, a conservative Southern state's righter, to the
Presidency.

Then, after Democrat James Polk had beaten them in 1844,
the Whigs returned to the war hero formula. Mexican War
general Zachary Taylor was an ideal choice, and in 1848 he
gave the Whigs their second—and last—victory.

But Taylor, like Harrison, died in office and the colorless
Millard Fillmore succeeded him in 1850. Fillmore capped an

ill-starred administration with his support of legislation to force the return of runaway slaves. That stand, which infuriated his northern supporters, was a death sentence for Whiggery. Little-known Democrat Franklin Pierce routed a final Whig military candidate—General Winfield Scott—in the election of 1852, and the Whigs never again could muster a serious threat.

Many historians have been unmerciful in their appraisal of Whiggery. The passage of time has made the Whig movement appear flabby, compromising, hypocritical, and devoted to nothing more than the seeking of office.

Yet, there must be something of value in any political movement powerful enough to elect an American President, and there was some value in Whiggery.

It was a way station for American Conservatism, a stopover between 18th Century Federalism and the Conservative programs which characterized both Republican and Democratic philosophy in the latter half of the 19th Century.

First of all, the Whigs were reacting against a man, Andrew Jackson, whom they believed to be the personification of all that was bad in unchecked popular tyranny. They were revolted by his ignorance and lack of polish, his disdain of tradition, his insistence that "to the victor belongs the spoils."

But there was more to the Whig movement than bare opposition. The Whigs believed America must return in some degree to the dignity and high-minded principles of the founding fathers.

American business was making prodigious strides, and it needed a voice in the government. The rising tide of anti-slavery feeling needed a voice, too. The Whigs offered some means for both expressions.

If it was a part of cynical compromise—of principles easily bent to accommodate the goals of many dissenting groups— it was such a party because that was the only way Whigs could muster a coalition strong enough to beat the Jacksonians. To them, it was compromise or accept defeat.

Modern Conservatives can learn some valuable lessons from the study of the rise and fall of the Whigs.

They can learn, for example, how weak a foundation for

political success is the principle of simple opposition, and how short-lived is this kind of success.

The Whigs were against Jacksonian democracy, but they were too engrossed in business as usual to formulate any effective alternatives.

They wanted a President of greater dignity and intellectual stature than Jackson could offer, but they passed up their best men in favor of war heroes who had a better chance to win.

They professed the high principles of Conservatism, but they compromised them at every turn in order to capture votes.

They built their house on shifting sand, and it collapsed before it had a chance to be tested.

THE REPUBLICANS

It was an angry throng which answered Allan Bovay's call to a protest meeting in the little Congregational Church at Ripon, Wisconsin, on March 1, 1854. They were Whigs, Democrats, Free Soilers, independents, and all with a common bond—outraged opposition to the Western extension of slavery as proposed in the Kansas-Nebraska Bill.

At first they were called "Anti-Nebraskans," but Bovay suggested another name to publisher Horace Greeley, and the name stuck:

Republicans.

Only a prophet with a crystal ball could have foreseen that this "band of rowdy rebels," as one newspaper account termed them, were laying the groundwork for the party which for the next century was to be an essentially Conservative one. Old-line Whigs looked with dismay on the radical spirit of the new Republican Party, and saw in its hot-headed sectionalism and anti-slavery pronouncements a direct road to civil war.

Whiggery was dying, and there was no really effective Conservative party operating. The men who followed John C. Calhoun were the most consistently Conservative political leaders of the 1850s. It was Calhoun, the unbending South Carolina Senator and Vice-President, who had spoken most effectively for individual and state freedom in an ordered

society—for the rights of minorities to be free from domination by popular majorities. Calhoun's passionate defense of
slavery is repugnant to most 20th Century Americans, but
his thoughtful declarations of Conservative principles are
still worth studying today.

But in the mid-1850s, when emotionalism ruled on both
sides of the Mason-Dixon Line and civil war was fast approaching, there was little inclination toward thoughtful reason. The overriding issues of Union vs. Secession, Slavery
vs. Abolition, obscured the traditional arguments of Conservatism vs. Liberalism.

The Republicans worked fast. They whipped together a
party organization and made a spectacular splash on the
national scene just two years after the Ripon meeting. Color-
ful John C. Fremont, the "Pathfinder," was their candidate
in 1856. James Buchanan and the Democrats won, but by
1860—with the opposition split three ways—they roared to
victory with that symbol of Union and rural honesty, Abraham Lincoln.

What was Lincoln's position in the Conservative-Liberal
spectrum?

The press of wartime problems which occupied him
throughout his four years and six weeks in the White House
make it difficult to assess that position. Conservatives of his
day considered him too Jacksonian for their taste. Moreover,
he assumed more powers for the Executive than the Constitution permits, and he arbitrarily stifled some freedoms which
in normal times should not be limited. But he was fighting
a life-or-death battle for the preservation of the nation itself,
holding off powerful Confederate forces on one hand and
almost overwhelming political opposition on the other. The
wonder is that he did not use his powers even more dicta-
torially than he did.

Certainly Lincoln was devoted to the conserving of all that
was best in American government. He loved the Union with
a burning passion. He revered the Constitution, and only
the dire emergency of civil war led him to take liberties
with it. He had deep sympathy for the common American—
as only a man reared in poverty can have it—but he believed that the way to better the poor man's lot was to clear

he way for his self-advancement, not in pulling down the wealthy to his economic level.

Lincoln was no Conservative in the sense that McKinley was a Conservative three decades later. But he believed in most of the basic principles which guide Conservatives today. Republicans revere him as the spiritual father of their party, and the strength and wisdom he brought to the Presidency have been pointed to with pride by GOP candidates from his day to this.

The Republican Party which Lincoln led died during the Civil War—in fact, even its name was changed to the "Union Party" in the campaign of 1864—and it was born again in a different form under Ulysses S. Grant during the tragic period of Southern Reconstruction. The radical Stalwarts under whose influence Grant fell were neither friends of Lincoln nor of Andrew Johnson, who tried to carry out Lincoln's program of reconciliation.

It was under Grant's administration that Southern bitterness against Republicans was so firmly rooted that it is only now beginning to dissipate after 90 years. It was under Grant, too, that America's mushrooming business and industry moved into the close alliance with the Republican Party that has been maintained ever since.

In those wild, booming postwar years, business needed hard money, high tariffs—and most of all, an absence of control from Washington. The Stalwart Republicans, determined to insure Northern prosperity, went along with just about anything business asked. With the Democrats branded in the popular mind as the "Party of Rebellion" (not to mention Rum and Romanism), and with moderates among the Republicans heavily outnumbered, the Stalwarts raced ahead almost unopposed to create the most stimulating kind of climate possible for the growth of the new American capitalism.

It was an era marked by spectacular development of national industrial might, by the birth of giant trusts, by Westward expansion, and by general prosperity. If working hours were long and working conditions appalling by modern standards, at least every American could cherish the great dream of becoming a millionaire through sheer hard work and a little luck.

But, as has happened before and since, too much uncontrolled power concentrated in the hands of a single group produced excesses which threatened the general welfare and sent the political pendulum swinging toward center again.

Growing social unrest, coupled with the exposing of corruption in the Grant administration, almost beat the Republicans in 1876. Democrat Samuel Tilden received more popular votes than Republican Rutherford B. Hayes, and only some questionable maneuvering of Southern electoral delegations put Hayes into the White House. Considerably sobered, the Republicans instituted moderate political reforms and economic policies, and at last took steps toward conciliating the beaten South and bringing it back to full participation in national government.

The moderate James Garfield kept the GOP victory string intact in 1880. Then, a few months later, an assassin's bullet made Stalwart Chester A. Arthur the new President. Arthur was expected to be securely in the pocket of the industrialists and political bosses, but he demonstrated admirable independence in working for both Civil Service reform and the harnessing of the runaway trusts.

Republican rule was at last ended in 1884, but not the unbroken reign of Conservatism. Winner Grover Cleveland had a reputation for government economy and Conservative policies in general, and he maintained that reputation in the White House. Although he gave way to a Republican Conservative, Benjamin Harrison, in 1888, Democrat Cleveland was back in the Presidency in 1892.

Despite the moderation of both Republicans and Democrats in this era, the social reformers were winning converts by the hundreds of thousands. James B. Weaver's Populist Party, with its promise of cheap money and socialist reform, so worried industrial leaders that many of them supported Cleveland over Harrison in 1892. They believed Harrison incapable of winning, and figured Cleveland to be a safe alternative.

Depression marred Cleveland's second term, but his 1895 deal with financier J. P. Morgan rescued the national credit with private capital. Prosperity returned, and Americans were even more convinced that their destiny lay in giving free rein to those who had so spectacularly built the nation's industrial power and kept the American standard of living climbing steadily upward.

The stage was thus set for the last administration of the 19th Century—that of William McKinley.

Ohioan McKinley, protege of Republican managerial genius Mark Hanna, has gone down in history as the personification of rugged individualism and business politics. McKinley supported high protective tariffs, hard money and freedom of business from government control. Under his administration, profits and prosperity climbed together. The individual was king. No one owed him a living, and he owed no man support.

In this situation the classical Conservative ideals of balanced power, of unlimited opportunity for all, of free competitive enterprise, began to be eclipsed by the concentration of wealth and power in the hands of the few.

Unrest began to grow, and the dissenters banded together behind the persuasive William Jennings Bryan, advocate of free silver and darling of the debtor. Bryan tried for the Presidency three times, and three times he failed. But the strength he mustered was a symptom of dissatisfaction that bubbled up through the otherwise placid waters of business prosperity.

On September 6, 1901, a bullet from the gun of a mentally disturbed anarchist cut McKinley down and signalled the beginning of the end for a long era of American business reign.

"That damned cowboy," as Hanna liked to refer to Theodore Roosevelt, was hardly the anti-business demon that industrial leaders feared he was. But he was destined to set up some barriers on the previously unblocked business right-of-way.

The 19th Century bowed out with business and Conservatism in full control of America's governmental machinery. For a century which had started with a liberal revolt under

Jefferson and moved on into the unchecked popular rule of the Jacksonians, the 19th had proved Americans to be basically Conservative after all.

They had drifted into the radical fringes of the left, and now were far to the right of center. But they had moved back toward center before, and they were to do so again.

The freedom granted to the leaders of business throughout the years following the Civil War had produced the mightiest industrial machine the world had ever known, but not without considerable suffering on the part of many who were trapped in the lower reaches of the mechanism.

Their voices were heard in the rise of trade unionism and in the radical programs of the Populists. The forces of protest did not overthrow Conservative rule, but they were able to smooth off some of the rough edges of the free enterprise economy and point the way to a better balance between Capital and Labor in the years ahead.

Liberals and Conservatives split on many an issue during the 19th Century. They clashed on the question of state sovereignty, on the extension of the vote, on hard vs. easy money, on the tariff. But traditionally individualistic Americans of all parties and political philosophies never doubted that a man should manage his own affairs and should prosper or suffer as the result of his own choices.

The issue of whether an all-powerful national government should threaten personal liberty and initiative, under the guise of providing security, was never seriously considered.

Americans would not start considering it until three decades after William McKinley was laid to rest.

VII.

■ TRIUMPH AND DISASTER

"America is now sauntering through her resources and through the mazes of her politics with easy nonchalance," wrote the college professor as the nation prepared to welcome the Twentieth Century. "But presently there will come a time when she will be surprised to find herself grown old—a country crowded, strained, perplexed—when she will be obliged to fall back upon her conservatism, obliged to pull herself together, adopt a new regimen of life, husband her resources, concentrate her strength, steady her methods, sober her views, restrict her vagaries—trust her best, not her average, members."

The professor was Woodrow Wilson.

Certainly there was nonchalance, high-spirited confidence in American institutions and American destiny, a simple trust that God was on our side.

In the carefree years between 1900 and 1917 there were few who bothered to join the thoughtful Professor Wilson in worrying about the future of a maturing America.

One man who did some worrying was young Theodore Roosevelt, who had been tossed the Vice-Presidency by the Republican leadership in 1900 to keep him out of mischief. A year later, William McKinley was dead and "Teddy" was in the White House.

Young, ambitious and disturbingly liberal in his public utterances, Roosevelt frightened Republican Conservatives with his views on regulating the trusts. What worried Roosevelt about the America of 1901 was that the free reign given business was encouraging monopoly and hobbling the very competitive system in which he believed.

"He was an individualist," wrote Francis Graham Wilson, "but he was an individualist who believed that positive action must be taken by the government in order to restore the freedom of the individual against the encroachment of the trusts. He was not against business, but against abuses in business practice."

Roosevelt lost no time in earning his title of "trust buster." In February, 1902, a suit was instituted under the terms of the long-unused Sherman Anti-Trust Act of 1890 against the Northern Securities Company—a combination of competing railroads. The monopoly was dissolved. Triumphantly, Roosevelt hailed the decision as a demonstration "that the most powerful men in this country were held to accountability before the law."

It was the first of many such anti-trust actions in his two administrations. Business was shaken by these suits, but not really hurt. Roosevelt was too strong a believer in a free economy and the inviolability of property rights to allow any lasting damage to be done to the business structure.

His dynamic leadership rallied small businessmen, farmers and labor to his banner, and he was able to weld millions into a new and more truly Conservative kind of Republicanism.

Roosevelt was so firmly in control by the end of his elective term in 1908 that he was able to name his successor—William Howard Taft. He saw in Taft a man who would continue his new Republicanism, but here he was doomed to disappointment. Within two years he was calling Taft "reactionary," and mapping plans to return to the political wars himself in 1912.

Return he did, under the Progressive "Bull Moose" banner. But he succeeded only in splitting the Republicans and opening the door for the election of Democrat Wilson.

Although Wilson talked much like the old-line Conservatives of both parties before his election, he soon demonstrated in the Presidency that he shared Roosevelt's Progressive views. He supported new controls over business, worked for social legislation, and later battled traditional American isolationism in an effort to build the League of Nations.

With Roosevelt out of the picture, the Republicans were having nothing to do with Progressivism. They nominated the stately Charles Evans Hughes in 1916 and came so close to electing him that Hughes retired on election night convinced e had triumphed. But the Wilson slogan, "He Kept Us Out f War," had enough appeal to win him a second term.

Six weeks after his inauguration, Wilson was before Congress asking for a declaration of war against Germany and he other Central Powers. American pride had been stung by German aggressions on the high seas, and the nation was behind Wilson.

But with victory in sight, Americans deserted their President in his campaign to make the nation a working partner n international government. Isolationist sentiment swelled back in a tide that defeated Wilson and kept the United States out of the League of Nations. His health broken by overwork and disappointment, Wilson served out the final months of his second term an invalid.

Now began that raucous, prosperous, carefree decade so accurately labeled the "Roaring Twenties." Internationalism and social reform were out of fashion, and Republican Warren G. Harding's 1920 campaign slogan, "Back to Normalcy," exactly suited the spirit of the times.

Factories were running full blast to fill the insatiable demand for radios, automobiles, and a thousand other newly-developed consumer products. The people had money in their pockets and the nation was satisfied to give business free rein.

Certainly Harding and the Republicans were willing to let business lead the way to new heights of prosperity. The jovial Ohio newspaper publisher was content to preside over the national joy, to keep government at a bare minimum, and to trust the judgment of the good friends he had appointed to his cabinet.

In the third year of his administration, Harding learned that some of those friends had not been worthy of his trust. Shocking reports of graft and impending scandal began reaching him in the summer of 1923. Returning shaken and disillusioned from a trip to Alaska, Harding fell ill and died within a few weeks, just as the scandals began to explode in the nation's press.

Fortunately for the Republicans, the perfect antidote for the poisonous situation—Vice-President Calvin Coolidge—

was ready to move into the Presidency. That tight-lipped symbol of New England integrity took control, dismissed the sinning Cabinet members, and quietly went about re-establishing national confidence in government.

So capably did he do his job, and so firmly was the nation convinced of the basic soundness of his free enterprise philosophies, that he and the Republicans rode to another impressive triumph in the elections of 1924.

On and on the era of dizzy prosperity went, until there was hardly a man in or out of government who was not convinced that the condition was permanent. Coolidge and his advisors carried Harding's non-interference a step further: they conscientiously worked at making the federal government smaller and less expensive.

Business was a success, Coolidge reasoned. Let it work out its own destiny and the welfare of the nation would follow.

A Teddy Roosevelt would have looked about and found much in the economic situation to worry about. For one thing, the farmers were not sharing, as a group, in the general prosperity. The new scientific management was tending to make the laboring man a cog in a vast production machine, stifling his old pride in workmanship. Moreover, there was widespread dissatisfaction among labor over its lack of effective power to bargain for a larger share in the fruits of the general prosperity.

Most alarming, however, was the irresponsible speculation which was sending stock prices soaring beyond any logical bounds. Postwar expansion in Europe was slowing as production caught up with demand, and there were signs that America's producers had caught up with the consumers, too. But none of this was reflected in the stock market, which scored gain on gain and showered speculators with gaudy paper profits.

Unless a firm and conservative hand applied the brakes soon, there was sure disaster ahead.

American history had taught the painful lesson many times before: that when any one segment of the economy or the government is given unchecked control—be it king, sovereign states, the aristocracy, the electorate, a dictatorial president, industrial monopolies—the freedoms and opportunities of other segments are sure to be curtailed. The certain result is suffering and retaliation.

Coolidge was lucky. The bitter fruits of postwar irresponsibility did not mature until eight months after he was safely out of the White House and his Secretary of Commerce, Herbert Hoover, was in.

On October 29, 1929, the top-heavy stock market collapsed with a roar that reverberated around the world. Too late, industry cut back production, credit was abuptly tightened, and speculation ceased. The shock was too much for the American economy, and the most terrible of all national depressions was on.

Few Americans over 40 will ever forget the privation and desperation of the early 1930s. Business leaders, the Republicans—and most of all Hoover—were blamed. And since business, the Republicans and Hoover were in power when it happened, they must be assessed a share of the blame. But the roots of the Depression extended back to World War I and the years immediately after it. It was a worldwide calamity, one which struck Europe first and spread with varying intensity to all the world powers.

The reaction to postwar overexpansion would have hit America hard no matter what party or what individuals were in power. But the blow might have been softened had business leaders adopted more responsible policies, and if government had been blessed with greater foresight. It might have been an easier blow, too, if the average American had not spent so wildly during the Twenties and had set aside more of his new earning power as security against the inevitable economic slowdown.

But Hoover was the man in charge in 1929-33, and a disillusioned America held him chiefly responsible for its misery.

To a man who had risen from poor beginnings to wealth and lifelong success as an engineer and public servant, the mounting abuse was particularly hard to take. But Hoover believed so firmly in the idea that the American economy had built-in recovery powers, and that government interference would only upset the national business cycle, that he stood steadfast against the pressures for massive federal overhauling of the economic machinery.

He labored night and day to rehabilitate the business community so that it might resume its control and lead the way to a new era of prosperity. Only in that direction—not in the more popular route of relief checks and government-made jobs—lay the hope of America, he was sure.

But this time the roots of depression were too deep, and the follies of the past decade too damaging, to permit hope for any rapid self-healing of the economy. By mid-1931, with the long-awaited business upswing still not in sight, Hoover decided that only by government intervention could he avert total economic collapse.

He succeeded in pushing the revolutionary $2,000,000,000 Reconstruction Finance Corporation Act through the Democratic Congress in January, 1932. Federal loan funds were made available by this act to finance new construction and get money circulating again. Through the Emergency Relief Organization, the releasing of government grain surpluses to the needy, and the stimulus of the Home Loan Bank Act and other legislation, Hoover began training the big guns of government on the strongholds of the Depression.

So it was that Herbert Hoover, apostle of nonintervention, became the first President to assume for the federal government the primary responsibility for pulling the nation out of a depression.

But by that time America was crying out for a change. New York's jaunty governor, Franklin Delano Roosevelt, offered nothing particularly revolutionary in the Democratic platform of 1932—except the repeal of the 18th Amendment —but his engaging personality won supporters by the millions.

When the election returns were in, Roosevelt and the Democrats had won a smashing victory. The rule of business was about to be supplanted by the rule of alphabetical bureaus, and America was to get its first taste of modern Big Government.

That the new theory of something for everyone—of relief from the hard realities of economic laws by federal decree—

night carry a high price tag in skyrocketing public debt and
oss of hard-won individual freedoms, did not warrant serious
ttention.

America welcomed Roosevelt and his New Deal with open
rms.

The story of FDR's celebrated "First Hundred Days" is
now an American political classic. For sheer energy and in-
ention, they have never been surpassed.

The nation wanted action—almost any kind of action—
nd Roosevelt supplied it with verve and superb salesman-
hip. It was shock treatment, and it felt so good that it left
lmost everyone cheering. Even the U.S. Chamber of Com-
nerce, encouraged by 20 bills inaugurated by the New Deal
o help business, extended its official congratulations to the
new President in May, 1933.

Few paused to take stock of where it all might lead.

NRA, WPA, PWA, AAA, CCC and a dozen other agen-
ies, financed by deficit spending, all had a share in the planning and controlling of various segments of national life. As a
means of jarring the economy out of its paralysis and re-
toring lost confidence, they had value.

As time passed and the nation started climbing out of the
Depression, there were those who waited for some sign that
he New Deal was ready to remove the crutches and let the
conomy walk once again on its own feet. But they were
loomed to disappointment.

Among the disappointed was Herbert Hoover, who recorded his misgivings about the permanency of New Deal
"emergency" measures in his 1934 book, *The Challenge to
Liberty*. The Depression, he said, had brought to light many
weaknesses in the organization of the American system—
weaknesses which had allowed some selfish business leaders
o oppress their fellow Americans.

"Abuses of Liberty through betrayal of trust or through ec-
nomic domination," he wrote, "whether they be called 'un-
air competition,' special privilege, monopoly, exploitation,
vicious speculation or the use of property to oppress others,
are all sins against the whole system and ideals of Liberty."

But, he pointed out, the remedies applied by the New Deal in its first year bore the seeds of a new kind of tyranny that was just as much to be feared. "The American system of Liberty has been challenged and the cry has gone up that these problems cannot be solved within its own philosophy, and within a frame of government which cannot infringe upon Liberty."

By 1936, Conservatives were both disenchanted and fearful. They saw socialism in the policies of the New Deal and predicted that nothing short of disaster could result from their continuance.

Casting about in desperation for a spokesman, Republicans chose mild-mannered Alf Landon, who had overcome the Democratic tide to win the governorship of Kansas. The 1936 GOP platform, strictly anti-New Deal in character, was a study in negativism. So completely did the platform and Landon fail to capture the support of voters that the Democrats swept to victory in every state but Maine and Vermont.

Republicans staggered from the crushing blow, and jubilant New Dealers were now more sure than ever that the nation was theirs.

The pump-priming which had started in Hoover's last year and had been dramatically stepped up under Roosevelt gave the economy only temporary energy. Hardly had FDR started his second term when a recession started the nation to worrying again.

In 1938 Republicans scored significant gains in both Congressional and gubernatorial elections. The new GOP faces of 1938 included several who were to assume high positions of leadership in the next two decades—Henry Cabot Lodge, Jr., and Leverett Saltonstall in Massachusetts; Raymond Baldwin in Connecticut; John Bricker and Robert A. Taft in Ohio; Harold Stassen in Minnesota. In New York, young Tom Dewey narrowly missed scoring an upset in the governor's race.

There was some talk of a Conservative resurgence. But inside Republican ranks the talk was more about picking a winner.

As the 1940 GOP Convention approached, Conservatives

saw their best hope in the outspoken anti-New Deal Senator Taft, while those who leaned more to the Liberal view liked Dewey. Neither faction could prevail, and in the confusion an Indiana lawyer named Wendell Willkie came out of nowhere to capture the Presidential nomination. Willkie was the symbol of the public-spirited private citizen challenging the political pros. His fresh personality and his willingness to declare his honest convictions won millions of friends, many of whom felt that two terms were enough for any President, and that the New Deal already had gone too far.

But, although Roosevelt had a battle on his hands for the first time in three campaigns, the man from Hyde Park won again. It was not only that Roosevelt's popular appeal was well nigh unbeatable; that increasingly powerful organized labor was solidly behind the New Deal; that the Democratic organization was more efficient than its opposition. It was becoming more apparent that Americans were willing to trade at least a part of their freedom and individualism for the economic security promised by the New Deal.

The debate over whether New Deal economic policies could produce lasting benefits was never settled. The recession which hit in 1937 was soon eased by the demand for production to meet the threat of war.

By 1938, Hitler had drawn Europe to the brink of conflict, and in September, 1939, World War II was on. The United States hoped to maintain neutrality, but prepared to fight. While draftees trained, the factories hummed and the fear of returning depression melted away.

Pearl Harbor put a damper on partisan political warfare for the duration. Although Dewey and the Republicans made a respectable showing in 1944, America chose to keep its commander in chief until the fighting was over.

Death finally removed Franklin Delano Roosevelt from the Presidency on April 12, 1945, with the final military triumph only four months away.

Senator Harry Truman replaced Henry Wallace as vice-president on the Democratic ticket in 1944 because party leaders feared Wallace's outspoken pro-Russian attitude might cost votes. From the November election to the death of President Roosevelt five months later, Truman had not been given a thorough briefing on either international or domestic affairs by his busy chief.

The suddenness of Roosevelt's passing and the realization of his own lack of preparedness gave the shaken Truman a becoming air of humility as he took over the Presidency.

"Pray for me," he beseeched newsmen on the day he entered the White House.

The humble Truman of April, 1945, had become the vitriolic "Give 'Em Hell Harry" by the time he opposed Tom Dewey in 1948. How he confounded the pollsters and the professionals of both parties by upsetting Dewey that year is a story which still makes Republicans shudder.

Truman's "Fair Deal" was in many ways more radically Liberal than even the New Deal. That little of his domestic legislative program was passed must be credited to a generally Conservative Congress elected in the postwar Conservative resurgence.

He was more successful in his internationalist programs. His "Truman Doctrine" assumed for the United States the responsibility for Western defense all over the globe. He fathered huge foreign aid programs, and under the Marshall Plan, America poured $12,000,000,000 into European recovery between 1948 and 1951 alone.

His conduct of the unpopular Korean War and his defense of security risks and "Five Per Centers" in his administration undermined Truman's popularity. As the 1952 elections approached, it appeared certain that the 20-year rule of Democratic Liberalism was nearly over.

In that 20 years the balance of power had shifted dramatically. Organized labor, once a struggling underdog, had forged ahead under friendly Democratic administrations and now wielded tremendous economic and political powers. Once-dominant business was now a bitterly complaining outsider. And the federal government, once so small and unwilling to referee the economic contest, was planning, controlling and dominating every facet of American activity.

Sensing certain victory, the Republicans had only to choose the standard bearer who would storm into the White House. The 1952 convention battle lines were drawn up between the often-disappointed Senator Taft, leader of the Conservative wing, and General Dwight D. Eisenhower, sponsored by Dewey and the moderately Liberal forces. Eisenhower's personal political philosophy was almost completely unknown. But he was the great American military hero of World War II, and his tremendous popularity made him a virtually certain winner.

Again Taft was passed over by his party. The master legislator who had done so much to enunciate and preserve Conservative principles in American government sickened and died a few months after Eisenhower's inauguration. His uphill battles for responsible labor legislation, his campaigns for fiscal sanity, and his long struggle against the continuing encroachment of the federal government against individual liberties will long serve as a model for all Conservatives.

His death in 1953 left the Conservative movement without an acknowledged leader.

Eisenhower's "Great Crusade" of 1952 promised a return to federal thrift and efficiency, an honorable conclusion to the Korean War, an end to the coddling of Communists in government. Again, America was ready for a change, and the popular general scored a landslide victory over Democratic Liberal Adlai Stevenson.

Eisenhower soon made good on his Korean War promise. He made improvements in federal government efficiency. He made the elimination of security risks a matter of his own personal concern. And for a time he was able to cut the costs of government—a development which was reflected in a 1954 tax reduction.

His creation of the Department of Health, Education and Welfare ran counter to Conservative thinking, and his appointment of California's Governor Earl Warren as Chief Justice of the Supreme Court drew criticism. His support of unabated foreign aid also disappointed many Conservatives.

But on the whole, Conservatives considered his administration so great an improvement over that of Harry Truman that they had little but praise for Eisenhower.

Then came the Congressional elections of 1954, which saw the Democrats making heavy gains. Many members of the Eisenhower administration saw in the elections results a popular demand to steer toward the left, and the President reluctantly agreed.

Federal spending and budgets started skyward again. The brief era of "Modern Republicanism", which differed only in degree from previous Liberal Democrat regimes, soon had voters wondering whether there was really much difference between the parties.

There was one important difference. The Republicans had Eisenhower, and the electorate voted him home an easy winner over Stevenson again in 1956.

But as budgets crept steadily upward and Eisenhower lent his support to a variety of federal aid programs, frustrated Conservatives were stung to outspoken opposition.

Senator Goldwater, who blasted Eisenhower's proposed $71.8 billion budget in 1957 and later termed Modern Republicanism "nothing more than a dime store New Deal," led the Conservative revolt. He was the Presidential choice of many Conservatives at the 1960 Republican Convention, and when Vice-President Richard Nixon won his easy first-ballot nomination, there was talk of forming a Conservative third party.

Senator John F. Kennedy's incredibly narrow victory over Nixon in 1960 reinforced the belief of Conservatives that a Republican candidate of more staunchly Conservative principles could have won.

Today the battle lines between Liberalism and Conservatism are more sharply delineated than at any time since the political upheaval of 1932.

The Great Debate rages on.

American Conservatism has undergone change since the dawn of the Twentieth Century. The "devil take the hindmost" philosophy of McKinley era individualists has been tempered by a realization that true Conservatism thrives only when economic opportunity is guaranteed to all Americans. The isolationist convictions of 1920 have been replaced by

appreciation of the need for America to play a leading
e in the affairs of a rapidly-shrinking world. The total
volvement in "business as usual" is giving way to a new
erest in government and a determination to develop work-
le Conservative alternatives to federal control.

But Conservative insistence on economy and efficiency in
vernment is as strong as ever. So is the conviction that
dividual responsibility and opportunity must never be sur-
ndered. So, also, is the trust in the Constitution, and the
verence for the principles which built this nation.

Conservatism is made of sturdy stuff. Its programs change
meet changing times, but the laws which undergird it have
t been amended in all the centuries since man first un-
rtook to govern himself.

3.

Conservative Positions for the 1960s

■

VIII.

■ THE ROAD TO FREEDOM

Having now considered what Conservatism is, and how it got that way during nearly two centuries of the American nation, it is time to examine Conservative positions on the major issues of the 1960s.

Conservative spokesmen have taken firm stands on each of those issues: federal government power, taxation, welfare, labor, education, the free economy, civil liberties, the Constitution, Communism, national strength, American foreign policy. Some of their more notable declarations will be quoted in succeeding chapters.

Undergirding Conservative positions on each of these issues is one theme: Freedom—freedom of the individual citizen, the businessman, the farmer, the wage earner, the teacher, the member of a minority group, the nation as a whole.

Four years before his death, Senator Robert A. Taft of Ohio, long the leader of Conservative forces, made this declaration of principles in a *Fortune* article:

"For a hundred years," he said, "the idea of liberty inspired all Americans, and they boasted of it until it became tiresome to every visiting foreigner.... But today many Americans and most people throughout the world have forgotten what it means. The limitations on liberty have grown until in many totalitarian states the substance of liberty has completely disappeared.

"What is liberty?

"It is freedom of speech and of the press ... but it is much more. It is the freedom of the individual to choose his own work and his life occupation, to spend his earnings as he desires to spend them, to choose the place where he desires to live, to take the job that fits him, whether some union official is willing that he get it or not. It is the freedom of the local community to work out its own salvation when it

has the power to do so. It is the freedom of cities, countie
school districts; the freedom to educate one's own childre
as one thinks best. It is the freedom of thought and exper
ment in academic institutions.

"It is the freedom of men in industry to run the
businesses as they think best, so long as they do not interfe
with the rights of others to do the same.

"Certainly there are limitations that must be impose
by the state to protect the liberty of others, more and mo
as our economy becomes complex. But a party that believ
in liberty will impose such limitations only to the extent th
they are absolutely necessary."

Senator Taft's declaration is just as valid a base for Co
servative positions today as it was in 1949.

It is usually easy to predict what the position of Conserv
tive spokesmen will be on any issue which comes before th
American people, because the principles which underlie tha
position are essentially unchanging.

Conservatives will line up consistently on the side of ir
dividual and state responsibility, and against enlarging th
scope of federal control; on the side of the free market, an
against economic planning; on the side of pay-as-you-g
financing, and against increasing the national debt.

And always Conservatives will stand for preserving free
dom.

But, Liberals often ask, what freedoms have we surren
dered?

Raymond Moley, in his book *How To Keep Our Liberty*
has a ready answer:

"The farmer has paid for his benefits by successive sur
renders of freedom. First, he accepted restrictions on hi
acreage. Then ... marketing quotas were established ... Th
farmer's financial affairs, including his credit and his debts
have to a degree moved within the jurisdiction of bureauc
racy.

"The worker's freedom has been restricted by the govern
ment alliance with his leaders ... His ambition to excel othe
workers finds impediments in union discipline ... Even hi

political rights have in some instances been ruthlessly suppressed.

"The businessman hardly needs to be reminded of the growing limitations on his freedom. The shrinkage of risk capital through taxation is met by inducements to become the debtor of a government bureau . . . Masses of regulatory laws, many of which have outlived their purposes, impose the yoke of bureaucrats on businesses.

"The citizen's right to keep or dispose of his savings has been greatly impaired by taxes and the inflationary spending of the welfare state. . . .

"Higher education in privately endowed institutions, long the true sanctuary of freedom, suffers from the invasion of statism. The income of such institutions is squeezed by heavier taxation of former and prospective supporters. Government grants for this or that are eagerly accepted by desperate trustees and administrators."

Freedoms *have* been surrendered by Americans, Conservatives warn, and in massive amounts. It is only because they have been surrendered so gradually that protests are not shouted more loudly, or by more people.

Alarm over the nation's drift toward statism and away from individual freedom during three decades of Liberal ascendancy has sent Conservative spokesmen scurrying to their storehouse of inherited wisdom for freedom-based alternatives to Liberal programs.

The more they review the words and deeds of past American statesmen, and the more they observe the chasm which separates today's Liberal philosophy from that which nurtured American greatness, the angrier they become.

One of the most angry of all is William F. Buckley, who devoted an entire book, *Up from Liberalism,* to a roundup of Liberal shortcomings.

"What has befallen us, that Liberalism should be the only approach to democratic government, mid-twentieth century?" he asks.

"And if what has befallen us is a historical imperative, with which we must necessarily come to terms, must we do so joyfully? . . . It may be that the waters are out and no human force can turn them back; but is it necessary, that 'as we go with the stream, we sing Hallelujah to the river god?'"

Buckley accuses Liberalism of being flabby, over-sentimental, impractical, eager to accept easy, short-sighted solutions.

"It is the chronic failure of Liberalism that it obliges circumstance," he writes in a discussion of typical Liberal solutions to today's problems.

"There are unemployed in Harlan County? *Rush them aid.*

"New Yorkers do not want to pay the cost of subways? *Get someone else to pay it.*

"Farmers do not want to leave the land? *Let them till it, buy and destroy the produce.*

"Labor unions demand the closed shop? *It is theirs.*

"Inflation goes forward in all industrial societies? *We will have continued inflation.*

"Communism is in control behind the Iron Curtain? *Co-exist with it.*

"The tidal wave of industrialism will sweep in the welfare state? *Pull down the sea walls!*"

Buckley believes that a deep distrust of the American people lies at the heart of the Liberal insistence on federal planning and control.

"It is not easy," he declares, "to understand the Liberal fear of the voluntary approach to society."

Like many another Conservative spokesman, Buckley feels that government tampering with economic laws only postpones and intensifies the distress of those involved.

If there is long-range technological unemployment in Harlan County, or any other, Buckley sees solutions in the voluntary moving or retraining of the jobless. If there is overproduction in farming or industry, let the demand for the product—or the lack of it—determine which producers will remain in the market and how much they will produce.

The government is doing marginal producers no long-lasting favor by subsidizing them into remaining in the market longer than it is economically feasible to do so, Buckley believes. When federal subsidies blunt the sharp prodding of economic necessity, the hard decisions to re-tool the factory —plant a different crop—prepare for a more marketable skill—are postponed.

The eventual result?

A new group of unwilling government wards who have lost the precious right of self-determination.

What is the basis of Conservative positions on America's role in a troubled world?

Again, freedom is the undergirding principle.

Why do Conservatives advocate a tough stand against the spread of Communism abroad or its infiltration of our proudest institutions at home? Because Communism has stifled individual freedom and initiative wherever it has taken control.

Why do Conservatives insist that America maintain a military capability second to that of no other nation in the world? Because there is no other way to maintain our freedom, and the freedoms of those nations which look to us as a bulwark against the Communist tide.

Why do Conservatives battle to keep American sovereignty unimpaired, and oppose surrendering any vital part of it to the United Nations? Because, important as the United Nations may be as a tool for furthering international understanding and cooperation, it must never be allowed to usurp this nation's freedom to act in its own best interests.

"Peace must be the ultimate aim of our foreign policy," stated Senator Taft in the *Fortune* article cited earlier, "and no other object is more important *except* the liberty of this nation itself . . . Unquestionably, we must join with other nations in any international organization that can effectively keep the peace. Because the United Nations organization itself is defective, and because of the attitude of Russia, we are justified in joining other groups with a more limited membership to keep the peace within the area of their jurisdiction.

"In order to protect our liberty and also to discourage others from attacking us, we have to maintain armed forces completely adequate for defense. . . .

"Under the present-day conditions, I believe we should continue our assistance to many nations to restore their economies from the disruption arising from the war because that disruption leads to the spread of Communism. . . .

"But let us not slip quietly into using our economic power to assume political power . . . It is easy to slip into an attitude of imperialism and to entertain the idea that we know what is good for other people better than they know themselves. From there, it is an easy step to the point where war becomes an instrument of public policy rather than the last resort to maintain our own liberty."

There it is—the sane and sturdy policy which has been the basis of Conservative stands on foreign relations since the end of World War II. It stresses liberty and peace, in that order of importance; participation in the United Nations, but a realization of UN shortcomings; strong military forces to discourage enemy aggression; assistance to other nations when such assistance blocks the spread of Communism; avoidance of imperialism; the recognition that war is a last resort to maintain our liberty.

The Conservative positions set forth in succeeding chapters are based, not on expediency—not on the postponing of economic distress for the sake of temporary prosperity—not on "peace in our time" at any cost—but on proven principles which have met the tests of centuries.

They are difficult, demanding positions, and they require the hardest kind of work and self-sacrifice. For their goal is freedom, the most precious of man's treasures and the most difficult to win and to keep.

IX.

▪ CAN THE FEDERAL GOVERNMENT REALLY DO THE JOB BETTER?

Their housing was miserably substandard.

Their schools were pitifully inadequate and their teachers underpaid.

There wasn't enough food, or enough medical care, and nearly half their number had died in the bitter cold and privation of the previous winter. No one was sure how much longer they could remain at peace with the potential enemy which outnumbered and surrounded them.

They had an easy way out of their difficulties—the good ship Mayflower, which rode at anchor in the bay, ready to take them back to the warmth and security of England.

But the Pilgrims, who had nothing to lean on but faith in God and their own ability, decided to stick it out.

They sent the Mayflower home.

Today, in some circles, such foolhardy individualism would be denounced. The Plymouth Colony would be proclaimed a "depressed area," and federal aid would be rushed in immediately. Low rent housing units would be built at once, and federally-financed school buildings would be constructed. A fair minimum wage would be established, and the government would offer to buy up, at a fair price, any produce which could not be readily sold. Federally-subsidized medical care would be provided.

If there was not sufficient money in the national budget to finance these humanitarian programs, the debt ceiling would be raised to accommodate them.

In short, the solution to Plymouth's problems—according to the prevailing Liberal philosophy of paternal centralized government—would be to shift them as soon as possible to the willing shoulders of the federal establishment.

But the Pilgrims had the old-fashioned notion that it was

better to work out their own destiny—even though it meant
back-breaking toil and privation for their families—than to
give up and take the easy way out. Fortunately for the
future of the New World, they stayed on and passed their
traditions of self-reliance down to succeeding generations of
Americans.

What is the Conservative stand on the role of the federal
government in the 1960s?

1. That a strong, efficient federal government is essential,
and that the legitimate functions of federal government are
conducive to the maintenance of a free, productive society.

2. That the legitimate functions of federal government
are defined in the Constitution.

3. That when the federal government is allowed to assume
powers beyond those granted by the Constitution, the powers
beyond those granted by the Constitution, the powers and
responsibilities of the states and their citizens are diminished
proportionately.

4. And, finally, that the continued surrender of powers to
the federal government will eventually undermine the self-
reliance of the individual citizen to such an extent that he
will be unable to manage his own affairs.

Senator John Tower of Texas, one of the newest Conservative voices on the national scene, believes the growing centralization of power can only lead to totalitarianism.

"Liberal extremists in positions of authority in government
see themselves as the ruling elite of a new order, a controlled
society," he says, "because they have no confidence in the
ability of Americans to decide for themselves . . . By gathering more and more power in the hands of the federal government, and particularly of the Executive Department, we are
moving closer and closer to what might be called a benevolent
dictatorship. And, benevolent dictatorships have a way of
becoming very unbenevolent."

House Minority Leader Charles Halleck of Indiana is convinced that most Americans still are willing to work out their
destinies without federal government help or direction.

"Our people do not want their lives ordered from Washing-

:on," he once told the Indiana Editorial Association. "They love economic liberty as much as they love social and religious liberty. They want to run their own businesses in their own way, without dictation and control from Washington. They want the profit system to prevail because they know that there is no substitute for that incentive to effort, and they know that the standard of living of the people as a whole is higher as the individuals produce more. All that our people ask is that equity and justice prevail, and they will undertake to carve out their own destinies in their own way."

Senator Karl Mundt of South Dakota often cites the American tradition of limiting federal power. In a recent newsletter to his constituents, he reprinted a statement made by Georgia Senator Benjamin Harvey Hill more than 90 years ago:

"There is a corporation we may all dread. That corporation is the Federal Government. From its aggression there can be no safety. . . . *Let us be sure we keep it always within its limit.* If this great, ambitious, ever-growing corporation becomes oppressive, who shall check it? If it becomes wayward, who shall control it? If it becomes unjust, who shall trust it? . . . I beseech you, watch and guard with sleepless dread that corporation which can make all property and rights, all states and people, and all liberty and hope, its playthings in an hour and its victims forever."

Liberals charge that Conservatives fear their federal government, and therefore fear the American people, since the people established that government. But here they miss the point entirely. Conservatives do not fear the federal government *as it was established by the founding fathers.* That government was established with enough limitations, checks and balances to keep it forever the servant of the people. What Conservatives fear is a federal government which is bursting out of its Constitutional bonds and assuming the powers and responsibilities of the states and the people.

In 1934, when Big Government had just begun to emerge, Herbert Hoover sounded a warning in his book *The Challenge to Liberty,* citing the dangerous tendency of federal government bureaucracy to perpetuate itself.

"No one with a day's experience in government fails to

realize that in all bureaucracies there are three implacable spirits," wrote the former President, "—self perpetuation, expansion and an incessant demand for more power. These are human urges and are supported by a conviction, sometimes justified, that they know what is good for us. Nevertheless, these spirits are potent and possess a dictatorial complex. . . . Power is the father of impatience with human faults, and impatience breeds arrogance. In their mass action, they become the veritable exponents of political tyranny."

Hoover was well aware of the tremendous pressures for expansion which exist in any government agency. He knew that every ambitious and conscientious department head seeks to build his program—take on new responsibilities, add new staff members, expand into larger quarters, press for a bigger operating budget. This is human and natural. But, cautioned Hoover, this very human tendency in government officials must be curbed if the federal government is to remain within its Constitutional bounds.

The legitimate functions of federal government were explained by Senator Strom Thurmond of South Carolina in a 1961 address:

"Under the plan of government inaugurated with the Constitution and adhered to substantially until well into the 20th Century, our National Government was charged principally with the responsibility to defend the lives and property of all citizens equally. This means protecting willing exchange, and restraining unwilling exchange; suppressing and penalizing fraud, misrepresentation, predatory practices; invoking a common justice under written law. Government's legitimate purpose, as contemplated by the Constitution, is to codify and then inhibit all destructive actions while leaving all creative and productive actions, including welfare, charity, security, and prosperity, to *citizens acting voluntarily, privately, cooperatively or competitively, as they freely choose.*"

Thurmond then discussed the Constitutional charge to the federal government to provide for the national defense, maintain internal order, and insure domestic tranquility.

"The government," he added, "was clearly conceived as an umpire, not as a participant, in the activities of society; it was conceived as an instrumentality to insure fair play and

he absence of fraud, not as one to guarantee the economic or
ocial success of individual or cooperative endeavor, nor as
ne to mitigate the burden created by the failure of such
ndeavor."

It is evident, then, that Conservatives view the federal
;overnment as a protector of individual liberty, not as a
isurper of it; as a guarantor of opportunity, not of security.

Tom Anderson, widely-read publisher of the *Mississippi
Farmer,* captured the essence of the Conservative view of
ederal government in this terse little definition of govern-
nent's new role:

"MOTHER HEN: A symbol of the federal government
..formerly known as the eagle."

And what is the Conservative stand on states' rights?

Conservatives revere the Jeffersonian concept of vigorously
ndividualistic states, solving their local problems, assuming
heir Constitutional responsibilities, and working together in
harmonious federal framework. They cannot agree with the
dea—once expressed by Jefferson—that national government
night well be "reduced to foreign concerns only," and that
he states would be relied upon for the competent adminis-
ration of all domestic affairs.

Conservatives see much to applaud in the declarations of
ohn C. Calhoun, who never ceased reminding his fellow
Americans that "when it was proposed to supersede the Ar-
icles of Confederation by the present Constitution, they met
n convention as States, acted and voted as States; and the
Constitution, when formed, was submitted for ratification to
he people of the several States." But few modern Conserva-
ives could support Calhoun in his theories of nullification,
r of a state's right to secede from the Union.

The Civil War settled the question of secession. But it did
tot erase state lines, nor did it change the Constitutional
rinciple of reserving all powers to the states and to the
eople which are not specifically granted to the federal gov-
rnment.

There is much more at stake here than state tradition and
ride. And there is more to the case for state powers than a

simple falling back on the argument that the Constitutio
provides for such powers. The Constitution can be changed-
and would be changed if enough Americans ever should d
cide that the rights of the states no longer were of impo
tance.

Americans need to remember *why* the framers of the Co
stitution were so insistent on protecting the rights of the i
dividual states to manage their own affairs to the greate
practical degree.

"There is a *reason* for the (Constitution's) reservation
State's Rights," declared Senator Barry Goldwater in *T
Conscience of a Conservative.* "Not only does it prevent th
accumulation of power in a central government that is r
mote from the people and relatively immune from popula
restraints; it also recognizes the principle that essentially loc
problems are best dealt with by the people most direct
concerned."

Who knows better than New Yorkers how much and wha
kind of publicly-financed slum clearance in New York Ci
is needed and can be afforded? he asked. Who knows bett
than Nebraskans whether that State has an adequate nursin
program? Who knows better than Arizona the kind of scho
program that is needed to educate their children?

How do Conservatives regard the role of the counties, th
cities, and the individual American in the government
the 1960s?

Consistent with the basic principle that all functions
government should be performed by the smallest unit capabl
of doing the job, Conservatives believe that local governmen
must assume an increasingly important role in today's Amer
ica.

It is in their local governments that citizens can take th
most direct kind of action. The work of one man or of a
energetic committee can, and often does, elect or defeat
county supervisor, a city councilman, a parks board director.

It is at this level that schools are supervised, hospital
erected, property taxes levied.

It is here, Conservatives believe, that all citizens mus

xercise their rights and their responsibilities to the fullest ex-
ent if the American ideal of self-government is to be
erpetuated. And it is here that Americans must reject with
tmost vigor the encroachments of federal authority.

This is why Conservatives battle so tenaciously against fed-
ral aid to education, and the federal controls over education
vhich would almost certainly follow. This is why Conservatives
ppose further federal intervention in the affairs of the cities,
s proposed in the plan for a federal Department of Urban
Affairs.

Here, on the local level, is where welfare should be ad-
ninistered, not only because welfare is essentially a commun-
ty problem, but because local financing and supervision of
velfare helps sharpen the individual's sense of responsibility
or the well-being of his neighbor.

The individual's charitable instincts are tragically dulled,
Conservatives believe, when his contributions to the welfare
of the needy are extracted by a far-distant federal govern-
nent and distributed impersonally by an agency over which
ne has no direct control.

Local problems should, and must, be solved by local
action, declare the advocates of the Conservative approach.

But, like so many Conservative routes, the way of local
elf-reliance is more demanding of individual initiative and
sacrifice. It requires a higher level of citizenship to take a
personal interest in better local schools—and to pay for them—
than to pass the responsibility on to the federal government.
It takes more will power to write out a check for the local
United Fund drive than to submit to a bigger income tax
bite to support federal welfare programs.

If Americans will not spend the time and the energy and
the money to solve their own local problems, however, they
can have no valid complaint if the federal government steps
in and solves those problems for them. Our children must
be educated, our needy cared for, and decent urban housing
made available.

The only question is: who is to do it?

The urban problem is a good example. In a thoughtfully
written book, *The Federal Government and Metropolitan
Areas,* written by Robert H. Connery and Richard H. Leach

and published in 1960 by the Harvard University Press,
is pointed out that 85% of America's population now lives i
metropolitan centers. The stampede to the city has create
monstrous problems in housing, air pollution control, freewa
construction, and a dozen other areas.

The campaign to establish a federal department to dea
with city problems has been waged since Philip Kates sug
gested it to President-elect Woodrow Wilson in 1912.

Connery and Leach discuss the arguments for a Departmen
of Urban Affairs: the heavy concentration of population i
cities, the need for cities to share in the making of govern
ment policy, the better coordination which could be achieve
by gathering all present urban programs into a single cabinet
level agency.

They point out the arguments against such a department
the invasion of local prerogatives by the federal government
the additional cost, the administrative tangle which would re
sult from a new department cutting across the jurisdictiona
lines of existing departments.

Then Connery and Leach reach their conclusion: "Thos
opposed to a department have the stronger case. . . . Perhap
the most that can be said for a Department of Urban Affair
is that discussion of the idea keeps the need for action wit
regard to urban problems before the public."

American City magazine has declared editorially that "Th
need for an overall . . . department . . . is much less than wa
the case (in 1912) This owing in part to the spread of the
council-manager form of municipal government . . . and to the
excellent aids rendered by national organizations."

In urban problems, as in so many others, Conservative
support local action over federal action. But, again, it is no
enough to oppose the Kennedy plan for a Department of Ur
ban Affairs. Workable alternatives must be developed, because
the problems of the cities are becoming more acute with
every passing year.

Can the federal government do a better job in solving the
problems of the 1960s than can the states, the communities,
and individual Americans?

That is the question which runs with unbroken consistency through the Liberal vs. Conservative debate.

Liberal spokesmen take the position that since business, organized labor, and modern technology are growing bigger and more complex with every passing year, federal government must grow bigger, more complex, and more powerful, too.

Conservatives answer that such a proposition is not based on sound reasoning.

"The *scope* of activities of the non-governmental segment of our society has not increased," argues Senator Thurmond in advocating the Conservative view. "Both the size and accomplishment of their undertakings *have* increased, but they still operate in the area of creation and productivity—the very area reserved to them when the Constitution was written. . . . The objectionable increase in size of the National Government is not the greater degree of *power* exercised in the area of its original assigned function as defender and umpire, but to the expansion of the *scope* of its functions into new areas originally reserved for individual, cooperative and competitive endeavor."

The enlargement of the scope of federal authority has made itself felt in increased regulation and the strewing of red tape across the land. Businessmen run an obstacle course of rules and reports. John Citizen is often so baffled by the ways of bureaucracy that he will go to great lengths to avoid doing business with the government.

And the farmer!

An illustration of his predicament is this incident, quoted by the *Phoenix Arizona Republic*:

Dairy farmer Jesse Stalker, Ravena, N. Y., had more orders for cream than he could fill from his own herd's production, reported Rep. R. Walter Reihlman (R-NY) in the *Congressional Record*. So he bought cream in 20-quart cans from outside sources. Then someone discovered that there is an Agriculture Department rule against buying cream in 20-quart cans. For his violation of this rule, Mr. Stalker lost his producer-handler exemption and was fined $20,899. According to Rep. Riehlman, the unlucky Mr. Stalker faced a choice between selling his dairy herd or mortgaging his farm to pay the fine.

Stories of the bureaucratic labyrinth, some hilarious and some tragic, fill many a book. There will be more, too, as federal government influence expands. For the planning and regulation of one area of productivity invariably leads to injustices in other areas. The result: More planning and more regulation.

It is like trying to wrap an octopus in tissue paper.

X.

ON TAXING AND SPENDING

The venerable Senator from Virginia rose from his seat with a trace of weary desperation, like a structural engineer who is about to warn an unheeding theater crowd for the 57th time that the ceiling beams are rotted and the roof may collapse at any moment.

The day was March 1, 1962, and Senator Harry F. Byrd was calling up before the Senate a measure known as H.R. 10050, which provided for raising the federal debt limit to $300 billion.

"A year ago," he said, "the previous Administration estimated a $1.5 billion surplus in the current fiscal year, 1962. . . .

"On March 27, 1961, the present Administration revised the estimate to forecast a $2.1 billion deficit.

"On March 28, the deficit estimate was revised to $2.8 billion.

"On May 25, the deficit estimate was revised to $3.6 billion.

"On June 27, the deficit estimate was revised to $3.7 billion.

"On July 25, the deficit estimate was revised to $5.3 billion.

"On October 29, the deficit estimate was revised to $6.9 billion.

"On January 18, 1962, the President in his budget message revised the deficit estimate again to $7 billion.

"The latest Monthly Treasury Statement showed an actual deficit of $9.4 billion during the first seven months of the year.

"Only last June 27, the Secretary of the Treasury testified that 'a temporary statutory debt limit of $298 billion should give us sufficient elbow room for maximum efficienc of operations.'

"Neither our form of government nor our system of en terprise can survive insolvency. All of us know that w cannot continue much longer to spend and spend, and ta and tax, and borrow and borrow. . . .

"In addition to $300 billion in direct debt, we have as sumed contingent liabilities at home and abroad amountin to untold billions more. Now we propose to underwrite th debts of the United Nations.

"It is possible to destroy ourselves from within. Nothin could serve Khruschchev better."

The magnitude of our national debt passed human com prehension years ago. Even one billion dollars is too vast sum to picture. A business could have lost a thousand dol lars every day—including Sundays—beginning 600 years be fore Jesus was born, and still not yet be a billion dollar in the red.

Three hundred billion? It is just a figure, an unsavory something to be skipped by hurriedly on the way from th sports section to the comic page.

Rep. Otto E. Passman of Louisiana has reported that the United States debt exceeds the debt of all other free worl countries *combined* by more than $100 billion.

And here is another shocker: In addition to our funde debt of $300 billion, we now owe $60 billion in unfinance pensions to retired military and civil employees, and we have promised to pay another $300 billion in veterans' com pensation and benefits. Add to that another $100 billion fo our unfinished construction and undelivered purchases. It al adds up to *$750 billion* in federal mortgages against the future.

How does such a staggering national obligation affect or dinary American citizens?

Well, for one thing, the *interest* paid on the funded deb in fiscal 1962 was more than $9 billion—which figures ou to $50 for each man, woman and child in the U.S., or $250 for each taxpayer with a wife and three children.

For another, as Senator Karl Mundt pointed out in a De cember 29, 1961, address, deficit spending has helped foster inflation to the point that the American dollar now has

eached a record low of 44.1 cents worth of purchasing
ower.

For a third, there is the demoralizing realization that our
children, and their children, are being saddled with debts
that they may never be able to repay.

As Senator Byrd points out, there are only two ways to
reduce this debt: By boosting federal income through higher
axes, or by reducing expenditures.

"But," says he, "we are already laboring under a terrible
tax burden—confiscatory in some areas . . . I do not see how
federal tax rates can be increased substantially. The point of
diminishing returns has already been reached. . . ."

The only alternative, then, is to apply the brakes to federal spending.

"It will be the individual responsibility of every Representative and every Senator," declared Senator Dirksen of
Illinois after the $300 billion debt ceiling was approved,
"to see that the ultimate in economy and thrift is exercised
to avoid being convulsed by an insurmountable debt."

But there has never been a shortage of brave resolutions
to reduce spending. Every national adminstration since 1932
has come to power swearing allegiance to the principles of
economy and balanced budgets.

Hear these words, delivered in solemn tones by Franklin
Delano Roosevelt during his 1932 campaign for the Presidency. In them, he took Herbert Hoover to task for—of all
things—spending taxpayers' money irresponsibly:

"The credit of the family depends chiefly on whether the
family is living within its income," FDR declared. "And that
is equally true of the nation. . . . But if, like a spendthrift,
it throws discretion to the winds, and is willing to make no
sacrifices at all in spending—if it extends its taxing to the
limits of the people's power to pay and continues to pile up
big deficits—then it is on the road to bankruptcy."

Having thus taken his position foursquare against deficit
spending, Roosevelt went on in a later 1932 campaign speech
to lash out against excessive taxation:

"Taxes are paid," he said, "in the sweat of every man

who labors, because they are a burden on production and can be paid only by production. If excessive, they are reflected in idle factories, tax-sold farms, and hence, in hordes of the hungry tramping the streets and seeking jobs in vain."

Brave words—and there is no reason to doubt that FDR meant them at the time. But history has shown how impotent they were, once the floodgates had been let down to provide "temporary" Depression relief. Once the flood of spending had started, there was no stopping it, even when the national economy was well on the road toward recovery. By 1935, federal expenditures were well over $6 billion. (Compare that with today's expenditures—approaching $100 billion.)

As the pace of spending mounted, and the debt along with it, there were many—even in the New Deal hierarchy —who began to worry.

William F. Buckley, in *Up From Liberalism*, gives his version of how those worries were laid to rest:

"At just that moment (midway in FDR's second term), an insight came to the rescue," he wrote. "Economists throughout the land were electrified by an alluring theory of debt that had grown out of the new, nationalistic economics of John Maynard Keynes. The ghost of the national debt was finally laid to rest! To depict the intoxicating political effect of the discovery, the artist of the *Washington Times-Herald* drew for the front page of his paper a memorable cartoon. . . . Dancing about him (Roosevelt) in a circle, hands clasped, his ecstatic braintrusters sang together the magical incantation, the great emancipating formula: WE OWE IT TO OURSELVES!"

Yes, we owe it—most of it, at least—to ourselves. But we owe it to millions of individuals who hold defense bonds, to life insurance companies whose government securities holdings guarantee the old-age independence of policy holders, to banks and savings institutions. Almost every American has some stake in that debt.

And it must someday, somehow, be repaid.

If any part of that debt were repudiated, confidence in the American government would crumble and the entire financial structure of the nation would come crashing to the ground.

National bankruptcy is more than a scary phrase. It has happened time and time again throughout world history, and the resulting devastation and suffering defied description. It can defeat and subjugate a nation just as effectively as can military defeat at the hands of an enemy.

"But how can we reduce federal spending in this era of Cold War?" people often ask. "Isn't most of it going toward national defense?"

Few Americans, Liberal or Conservative, are willing to scrimp on national military preparedness. But the truth is that *less than half* of the $95.8 billion appropriated by the 87th Congress in 1961—$46.7 billion, to be exact—went to the Department of Defense, according to figures published by the Congressional Quarterly Service.

Moreover, non-defense spending is increasing far more rapidly than is defense spending.

From 1954—the first year after the end of the Korean War—to 1960, national defense expenditures *declined* $1.3 billion, Senator Strom Thurmond reports. "During the same period, however, non-defense budgeted expenditures of the National Government rose $9.5 billion. . . . These figures show emphatically that the increased role of government is not, as many would have the public believe, due to the increased costs of adequate military strength," Senator Thurmond adds.

Where, then, is the money going?

The Congressional Quarterly Service score sheet for 1961 gives some answers: Agriculture, $5.9 billion; Labor-Health-Education-Welfare, $4.9 billion; Public Works, $3.9 billion; Treasury-Post Office, $5.3 billion; Foreign Aid, $3.9 billion; Independent Offices, $8.9 billion; Permanent Funds (mostly interest on the debt), $9.2 billion.

"New civilian jobs are being added to the Federal payroll at the rate of some 11,000 per month," reported Senator Karl Mundt on September 4, 1961.

New federal jobs and new federal programs do not account for all the increase. "In making up the 1961 budget, we found that built-in increases came to more than $2 billion dollars," reported former Budget Director Maurice Stans, "and looking ahead to the next budget, we see even now the prospect of another billion dollar increase in built-in items."

Obviously, we will have increased budgetary pressures even without adding a single new spending program.

Who pays this staggering bill for federal government each year?

One of our cherished beliefs is that—because of the graduated income tax—the wealthy pay a major burden of the cost of government. It is true enough that the graduated income tax does "soak the rich"—as much as 90 per cent of income in the highest brackets. But, as Senator Goldwater points out, "the total revenue collected from income taxes beyond the twenty per cent level amounts to less than $5 billion—less than the federal government now spends on the one item of agriculture."

So, apparently, the wealthy cannot pay much more, even if all incomes in the higher brackets were confiscated by taxation.

Perhaps it is the big corporations, then, which are paying the bill.

But listen to Congressman Wright Patman of Texas, former chairman of the Joint Congressional Economic Committee: "All of the experts who have studied this problem agree that a large part of the corporate income tax is shifted.... The giant corporations pay little, if any, of the tax. They simply treat the tax as an item of cost, set prices to yield the after-tax profits which they wish to make."

Corporations have no other choice. They must pay the market rate of return on investment if they are to obtain the capital funds with which to operate. An illustration is the comparison of corporation income taxes and corporate investment return since the mid-1920s: Between 1925 and 1929, corporation income tax rates varied from 11 to 13.5 per cent, and net return on stockholder investments averaged 5.62 per cent. Between 1952 and 1956, the corpora-

business which has a gross product valued at $30,000 a year. A pays B $20,000 a year to operate the business. That $20,000 is paid out of the $30,000. B furnishes the brains for the work. However, B employs C to do the actual work in producing the product, and pays C $10,000 for his services

We then add up all of these figures and we see that there is a total of $60,000. That amount is a part of what we call the gross national product. We see, however, that everything involved could not possibly exceed $30,-000, which was the product that was sold. Therefore, it is very deceiving to talk about the gross national product, is it not?

MR. BYRD. The Senator is entirely correct; gross national product figures can be deceptive, indeed.

MR. ERVIN. What we are doing is adding the money time and time again. Every time the money changes hands from one person to another, we have exactly the same amount of money, but we count the same money time and time again.

MR. BYRD. I thank the Senator. We have been depending entirely too much on possible increase in the gross national product as a basis for increasing expenditures of the Government.

That enlightening little conversation shows how shaky is the foundation upon which we are building our new spending programs. Suppose that the Mr. A in Senator Ervin's example finds that he must halt production because of slackening demand, declining profit margin, or for any other reason. Suddenly the $30,000 product is gone—and so is the $30,-000 in salaries paid to Mr. B and Mr. C.

As if by magic, $60,000 worth of gross national product has disappeared.

But does the total of government spending fall in the same proportion? It does not.

The yardstick of gross national product has its value as one means of measuring our economic growth. But it can change pace and direction faster than we can change national spending policy. Too much reliance upon its continual rise can lead us to financial disaster.

What do Conservatives propose we do to halt our national flirtation with bankruptcy?

Some Conservatives, like Representative Charles Halleck of Indiana, urge that the skyrocketing rate of increase in federal spending be reduced to a rate more in keeping with national economic growth.

Others, such as Senator Goldwater, demand more drastic action.

"The root evil is that government is engaged in activities in which it has no legitimate business," he said in *Conscience of a Conservative*. "The government must begin to *withdraw* from a whole series of programs that are outside its Constitutional mandate—from social welfare, education, public power, agriculture, public housing, urban renewal, and all the other activities that can be better performed by lower levels of government or by private institutions or individuals.

"I suggest that we establish, by law, a rigid timetable for a staged withdrawal. We might provide, for example, for a 10 per cent spending reduction each year in all fields where federal participation is undesirable."

But neither a moderate nor an abrupt slowdown in the rate of federal spending will be achieved without effort or sacrifice. If every member of the Administration and every member of Congress should decide tomorrow to reject every *new* spending program, the built-in cost increases in programs *already in effect* would keep federal budgets climbing for years to come.

What can each individual American do about getting his country back on the road to a sound financial policy?

For one thing, we can write our Senators and Representatives, urging them to vote against increased spending. Nothing affects their actions as much as a concerted protest from home.

For another, we can study their voting records, and with our votes replace the big spenders with men who are pledged to government economy.

Liberal spokesmen frequently declare that ever-increasing budgets and debt ceilings are inevitable—an irreversible trend of the Twentieth Century. The necessity for huge defense expenditures, the new demands of the Space Age, and the osts of our world-wide struggle with Communism make balnced budgets unwise and even impossible.

Conservatives answer that these new demands on our reources make it even *more* imperative that we reduce all ther expense to a bare minimum.

Conservatives know that all our efforts to keep the nation trong can go down the drain if inflation continues to shrink he dollar, and if America spends herself into bankruptcy. They know that an America crippled by economic collapse vill surely lose the life-or-death battle with Communism.

The milestones in budgeted federal spending which we have passed in only three decades are these:

1930 — $3 billion.
1940 — $9 billion.
1950 — $40 billion.
1960 — $80 billion.

"How long can the Federal Government continue to spend, ax, and borrow at the present rate?" asks Senator Byrd.

"Are we on a permanent deficit basis?

"When will the breaking point come?"

XI.

■ TO PROMOTE THE GENERAL WELFARE

Two American communities, as far apart philosophically as they are geographically, hit the front pages of newspapers across the land in mid-1961.

How Newburgh, N. Y., and Wink, Texas, went about solving their local problems makes an interesting case study in the Conservative vs. Liberal argument on today's looming Welfare State.

Newburgh (population 31,000) had a knotty relief problem. As City Manager Joseph Mitchell put it, "Ninety-five per cent of the population is spending *one-third* of its municipal revenue ($3 million per year) to support five per cent of the population."

Newburgh decided to tighten up on relief payments. Some of its relief recipients, it was found, were receiving more than some city employees. So a 13-point program was drawn up to help correct the situation.

Among the provisions: that all able-bodied adult males on relief should be put to work for the city; that, where possible, cash payments should be converted to vouchers covering food, clothing and rent; that all mothers of illegitimate children should be advised that, should they have any more children out of wedlock, the mothers would be denied relief; that all physically able relief recipients should be denied relief payments if they refused a job; that the allotment for a family unit should not exceed take-home pay of the lowest paid city employee with a family of comparable size.

The Newburgh proposals raised a storm of protest, both in Albany and Washington, and the city was threatened with withdrawal of welfare funds.

"So withdraw them," Newburgh's stubborn City Fathers replied. "We'll handle our own relief problems without outside help."

The Wink, Texas, story was a far different one.

Wink, once a booming oil town of 20,000, had dwindled o 1,863 souls as employment opportunities declined. So the own went to the federal government for aid. Uncle Sam, hrough the Urban Renewal Administration, did not disap- oint Wink. A grant of $891,868 was approved, along with $1,034,758 low-interest loan—a total of $1,034 per resident or restoration of a declining town.

The *Houston Chronicle* noted that, if the same formula vere used for Houston, the city would receive $969,118,446. "This fantastic project may do some good in the long run," he *Chronicle* editorialized. "It may point up for Congress the vhole problem of urban renewal and cause a reassessment f the program."

Newburgh got nothing for its efforts but charges of "lack f humanitarianism." Wink got a fantastic windfall.

Surely, the way of Conservatism is not always a happy ne.

Americans are among the most generous, compassionate eople on earth. No other people in the world are so quick o answer a call for charitable action, so eager to help a ellow human being in need.

In no nation is there less necessity for calling in the re- ources of the central government to care for the victims of ircumstance.

But it is because Americans are generous by nature that dvocates of the Welfare State have made so much headway n the past three decades. We find it all but impossible to urn down a federal proposal that offers help for the aged, he sick, the jobless.

In our eagerness to help those less fortunate than our- elves, we too often refuse to think through the question of ow that help may best be rendered.

"How easy it is to reach the voters with earnest impor- unities for helping the needy," says Senator Goldwater. "And ow difficult for Conservatives to resist these demands with- ut appearing to be callous and contemptuous of the plight of less fortunate citizens. Here, perhaps, is the best illustration of the failure of the Conservative demonstration. . . .

"I feel certain that Conservatism is through unless Conservatives can demonstrate and communicate the difference between *being concerned* with these problems, and believing that the *federal government* is the proper agent for their solution."

Here is the heart of the dilemma which confronts Conservatives when they face up to the question of welfare.

They know that it is better to provide for the needy through private means, individual or cooperative, or by local government programs. They know that the "bread and circuses" formula, through which Rome and many another nation were led to destruction, is a policy of disaster.

But how does one resist the call to federal "humanitarianism," transparently faulty though it may be?

The first thing to remember is that there is nothing humanitarian about pushing a free nation down the road to dependency on government. It does not require any particular humanitarianism on the part of a Congressman to vote for a bill which takes a certain number of Mr. A's dollars and gives them to Mr. B, especially when Mr. A may have his own ideas about how he wants to assist those less fortunate than himself.

And there is nothing humanitarian—or even moral—about shifting the responsibility for paying the massive welfare bill to future generations by means of deficit spending.

The Welfare State does not rush in. It creeps.

Today's emergency relief fund becomes tomorrow's permanent welfare program. Today's federal "gift" becomes by next year a benefit demanded and taken for granted. And wherever government money goes, government control must inevitably follow.

Sooner or later, Conservatives believe, federal paternalism weakens the determination of individual citizens to care for themselves and their needy neighbors. First, the urge to be charitable is dulled by the knowledge that the government will provide. And, eventually, increasing taxes gobble up the dollars which once went to private charity.

In the end the Welfare State holds full sway. Citizen

become wards and dependents, and the power of the government is as absolute as in any medieval dukedom.

There are those among the philosophers of Liberalism who welcome the Welfare State.

Arthur M. Schlesinger, Jr., the former professor and historian who now serves as a Presidential assistant, was quoted by United Press International on January 31, 1961, as saying that "a welfare state is the best defense against Communism, and a welfare state is one which provides basic elements for its citizens such as food, clothing, shelter, education and opportunity."

Conservatives reject such reasoning with all possible vigor. This is not the kind of America envisioned by those who founded this nation, nor is it the kind of America desired by a vast majority of citizens today.

The philosophy of welfare which guides most Conservatives in the 1960s includes these beliefs:

1. That a government which offers a maximum of freedom and opportunity will create an economic climate in which want and need are minimized.

2. That when circumstances do cause need, the victims are best helped by private means.

3. That when private aid cannot meet the need, assistance from local and state agencies can alleviate want without the danger of accumulating the vast political power which smothers freedom.

4. That public assistance should be as temporary an expedient as possible, and that no American citizen should be allowed to become a government dependent so long as he can provide for himself.

One of Liberalism's goals for the near future is the passage of legislation which would add medical care for the aged to present benefits under Social Security.

After the Forand Bill was repudiated by a 2-to-1 margin in the House Ways and Means Committee in 1960, its advocates shifted their support to the King-Anderson Bill. This bill, which resembles the Forand proposal in many respects, calls for levying an additional 1/4 of 1 per cent in Social Security taxes in order to finance hospital and nursing care

for persons eligible for Social Security old-age assistance. I
was introduced early in 1961 in both houses of Congress
but never mustered enough strength for passage.

Meanwhile, the 1960 Kerr-Mills Bill won the support o
many Conservatives, and it became law in that year. I
increased federal matching grants to the states for existin
old-age assistance programs, thus leaving to each state th
decision as to who would be eligible for aid, and how much

The American Medical Association, a bitter foe of th
Social Security approach to medical care for the aged, backe
the Kerr-Mills Bill. "We believe it maintains the fundamen
tal American philosophy of individual initiative, local deter
mination and local control," declared AMA President-elec
Dr. Leonard Larson in 1960. "We support it wholeheartedly."

Meanwhile, many plans for privately-financed old-age
health insurance programs have been developed, and man
employers, labor unions, and associations have put such plan
into effect.

Recently a bill was introduced in the House by Rep
Frank T. Bow of Ohio, providing for a voluntary plan o
medical care under which an aged person could finance hi
own health insurance, in part, by means of an income ta
credit. A relative or employer could receive a similar ta
credit by purchasing health insurance for a person over 65.

By such plans as these, Conservatives hope to solve th
very real problem of medical care for the aged without re
sorting to federal medical care, which would open the doo
to Socialized Medicine for all.

The entire field of Social Security legislation has bee
under Conservative fire for many years.

"There are two generic grounds for disapproving federa
social security—one economic, the other philosophical," de
clared William F. Buckley in *Up From Liberalism*.

"1. Social Security funds are not segregated against futur
withdrawals, but the assumption is that, at some future date
as much money will be flowing into the Treasury in pay
ments by subscribers to Social Security as will leave th
Treasury to meet obligations. . . . The more serious economi

case is based on the certitude of inflation. Dollars paid today will be repaid 40 years from now, but will be worth less. . . .

"2. Philosophical grounds: a—Blanket Social Security coverage encourages malingering and abuse, encourages idleness instead of mitigating hardship; b—Social Security laws are an imposture—they are put forth as 'insurance,' but they are not; c.—Social Security programs are redistributionist in character, they take money from some and give it to others; d,—Compulsory participation is wrong—it diminishes human freedom, forces men to give up part of today's rewards by government decree 'for their own good.' "

No private insurance company would be permitted to operate a program as Social Security is being operated. Payments by individuals and employers are not being kept aside to pay benefits when they come due. And Social Security is running in the red.

Most Americans are convinced that they and their employers are paying the full cost of their own old-age benefits. But it simply isn't true.

"When the fraudulent but now prevalent assumption that people pay directly for their own benefits (under Social Security) is abandoned in the name of honesty, Congress should see that pension costs are bearable," wrote Raymond Moley in *How To Keep Our Liberty.* "That should mean that no one would receive pensions as a matter of right. The basis should be one of need."

Social Security is firmly established in the American pattern today, however, and there is little likelihood that it will be dislodged. One reason for its popularity has been the knowledge on the part of the worker that his employer is being assessed for part of his retirement income. But, as in the case of corporation taxes, the employer merely passes his share of the bill along in the form of higher prices for his products. The result is more inflation.

And, with the blunting of the once-sharp necessity to save for their old age, Americans are less likely to build up a financial cushion for their later years.

The more government tries to provide old-age security, Conservatives believe, the greater is the temptation for individuals to let the government do the job.

Another difficult welfare problem is that of unemployment compensation. Here, again, the primary Conservative goal is to solve the problem at its source by creating more jobs through the encouragement of business and industrial growth.

But there will be some unemployment in even the healthiest economy. The move toward industrial automation—although it is likely to provide more job opportunities in the long run—causes temporary unemployment. Our fast-changing technology makes some job skills obsolete while it creates shortages in others. For these and many other reasons, America is likely to have several million unemployed workers at any given time in the foreseeable future.

To alleviate the hardship of unemployment, there should be some form of temporary compensation to tide a family over until the breadwinner is able to get another job.

Conservatives recognize this need. They want to keep compensation on a state and local basis, however. And they want to be sure that any such compensation plan does not become a haven for those who simply do not like to work.

For this reason, Conservatives usually oppose moves to lengthen compensation periods, increase payments, and add new benefits. Unemployment compensation, they believe, should be designed to relieve hardship—not to provide a permanent home on easy street for the welfare chiseler.

A plan to reduce chronic unemployment by retraining certain hard-to-employ workers was introduced in Congress by the Administration in 1961. Conservatives did not like its "shotgun" approach, which did not clearly define what skills these workers were to be trained for.

So Conservatives suggested changes. They insisted the bill set specific requirements, list skills desired, provide for participation and financial support by each state. When Rep. Charles Goodell, New York Republican, submitted his bill embodying the Conservative changes, it passed the House of Representatives on February 28, 1962, by a 352-62 margin.

Even the Administration was happy. Secretary of Labor Arthur Goldberg said the bill "will arm the nation with a powerful new weapon to help alleviate long-term unemployment."

The principle is one Conservatives can cheer. Certainly it is better to retrain workers for future productivity than to pay them for remaining in idleness indefinitely.

An Administration proposal to create a Youth Conservation Corps, reminiscent of the Civilian Conservation Corps of Depression days, is not likely to receive as kind treatment at the hands of Conservatives.

Senator Mundt explains why:

"This is an idea to relieve unemployment and help conserve some of America's natural resources. The first year, 30,000 YCC enrollees would participate in the program. This would only cost something around $3,600 per enrollee, or, according to the Bureau of the Budget, $120 million.

"But the program doesn't stop at the $120 million point. For the second year, there would be 50,000 people in the YCC, upping the annual bill to $200 million. At the end of the third year the YCC would be doubled, hitting a strength of 100,000 (costing $400 million a year). In the fourth year the number of enrollees would move up another 50,-000. . . . At the end of five years you would have a program costing nearly TWO BILLION DOLLARS, but—and note this—with OVER 60 per cent of the total cost coming in the LAST TWO YEARS!

"Which simply goes to show that, while the donkey's eyes may attract your admiration, it's the kick in the end that hurts!"

New proposals to give some segment of the American citizenry another "free" benefit, at federal expense, are introduced in Congress almost daily. If any appreciable percentage of them became law, national bankruptcy would have overtaken us long ago.

How much better it would be for America, Conservatives believe, if half the energy expended in developing these give-away proposals—and in lobbying for and against them —could be channeled into the job of making our private welfare systems work!

The United Fund provides a good example of what can be done when people lose their obsession for letting the government do it, and resolve to help each other on the local level.

According to a November 4, 1961, *Saturday Evening Post* editorial, 18 million unpaid men and women in 2,200 local United Fund organizations raise more than $500,000,000 each year for families in distress, for orphans, the sick, the handicapped, the aged, and for youth and community projects.

"A nationwide voluntary movement to relieve suffering and save lives, it is a striking demonstration of the brotherhood of man," concludes the *Post*.

If the billions in taxes now extracted from the people for federal welfare programs were given voluntarily to private charities—churches, community funds, labor union charities, and the like—operational costs would be reduced, and the needy would receive far more help than they now do. More important, the ominous threat of Welfare Statism would be forever removed.

"But individuals and private organizations cannot, or will not, do the job," the Liberal spokesman argues. "Only through the federal government can we give enough help to those who need it."

Until all Americans resolve to give through private charities—and to give enough to do the job—the pressures for government intervention will continue.

"Socialism-through-Welfarism poses a far greater danger to freedom than Socialism-through-Nationalization, because it is more difficult to combat," declared Senator Goldwater in *Conscience of a Conservative*.

"The evils of Nationalization are self-evident and immediate. Those of Welfarism are veiled and tend to be postponed. . . .

"The effect of Welfarism on freedom will be felt later on—after its beneficiaries have become the victims, after dependence on government has turned into bondage, and it is too late to unlock the jail."

XII.

■ FREEDOM FOR THOSE WHO LABOR

Karl Marx—if he could return to earth for a peek at America in the 1960s—would be crushed.

He had worked out such a dynamic plan for the future: The oppressed working class was to rise in its fury and overthrow the owners and manipulators of capital. Nothing was so vital to Marx as the class struggle, and the proletariat was to stop at nothing in the waging of it.

Today, Marx might find the steamfitter from the local plant tuning up his outboard motor in anticipation of a weekend at the lake, where his cottage adjoins that of the branch bank manager.

He might find men working at the transistor factory on a Saturday afternoon, but the draftsman would be drawing time-and-a-half, and his boss would be working late in the office upstairs in the hope of landing a big contract come Monday morning.

He would find stock certificates in the union man's safe-deposit box, and he would find bosses often putting in longer hours than the help.

Karl Marx would, in short, find so many capitalists laboring, and so many laborers sharing in the fruits of capitalism, that he would soon despair of separating them.

How could a self-respecting reformer promote a class war in an atmosphere such as that?

The labor union movement has been a potent force in bringing about the conditions under which the American working man shares in the national productivity as no other laboring man has shared before.

No true Conservative is anti-labor, because "labor" in its broadest sense includes almost everyone who works for a living.

Nor are Conservatives anti-union.

"Unions can be an instrument for achieving economic justice for the working man," a prominent American has declared. "Moreover, they are an alternative to, and thus discourage, State Socialism. Most of all, they are an expression of freedom . . . an expression of man's inalienable right to associate with other men for the achievement of legitimate objectives."

Was this George Meany talking? Walter Reuther? No, the speaker was Senator Goldwater, whom Liberals malign as the most "anti-labor" of all Conservatives.

But Senator Goldwater is not anti-labor.

What he and most other Conservatives object to in today's labor picture is the awesome *power*—both economic and political—which is now concentrated in the hands of a few union leaders.

There was a time, during the heyday of the industrial and financial trusts, when the shoe was on the other foot.

In that era, when "elephants and ants were free to step on each other," as Gordon Harrison put it, the giants of industry strode the land almost unchallenged. Their influence on the course of government and the lives of all Americans was tremendous. A monopoly maneuver could wipe out a small businessman almost overnight. Great segments of the population were under their economic domination.

The political power of Big Business was apparent in the number of Congressmen controlled, and in such statements as that of one factory owner to his employees in 1896: "If Bryan wins over McKinley tomorrow," he warned, "there will be no jobs for you here the day after."

But an aroused citizenry struck back with anti-trust legislation. The trusts were broken up, and free competition was allowed to function again.

These same anti-trust laws, however, have never been applied to labor unions.

Today, it is unlawful for corporations to combine in the setting of industry-wide prices, but labor unions may establish industry-wide wage levels and terms of employment.

In all but 19 states, union membership may be demanded as a requirement for employment.

And in all states, union leadership may extract from each

member's pay a contribution to COPE—the AFL-CIO Committee on Political Education. The money thus collected is used to elect government officials friendly to the unions. It makes no difference that an individual worker may favor an opposition candidate. His money is used to elect the man whom the union leadership prefers.

COPE has been a huge success. Even before the election of the Kennedy Adminstration in 1960, according to figures published in a COPE political memo, the organization was instrumental in electing 62 per cent of the House of Representatives, 77 per cent of the Senate, and 74 per cent of the nation's governors in 1958.

In the first six decades of the Twentieth Century the economic power of Big Business has been effectively neutralized—through enforcement of the Sherman Act and later anti-trust legislation. At the same time, Big Labor's powers have steadily grown—aided by the Wagner Act, the Norris-LaGuardia Act and similar legislation—until union leaders now wield power approaching that which once was in the hands of the giants of business.

Conservatives have traditionally mistrusted heavy concentrations of power, in any segment of the economy and in any branch of the government. It is just such concentration of power in the hands of labor union leadership that Conservatives oppose today.

What is the Conservative position on compulsory unionism?

In the first place, it might be argued, unionism is not compulsory in the United States. No worker is forced to join a union—unless he wants to work in a plant where a union shop contract is in effect. But, obviously, this is about as compulsory a situation as can be imagined if the worker happens to live in an area where his skill is used only by plants with union shop agreements.

So union membership, in many millions of cases, is compulsory if the worker and his family hope to eat and maintain a home.

Generally speaking, Conservatives believe that a man

should have the right to join a union—or not to join one—as he sees fit.

The freedom to associate with other men in a cooperative effort to achieve worthy goals is a right which Americans have enjoyed for centuries. So is the right *not* to associate. The staunchest union advocates will argue for these rights in every area except that of unionism.

But unionism is a special case, they explain. Organized labor's gains have been won only by presenting a united bargaining front, and if some workers are allowed to remain out of the union, the united front will be weakened and management will soon become dominant again.

It is easy to understand why union leaders want compulsory membership. Any association, no matter for what purpose it is formed, would be stronger and do more for its members if membership could be made compulsory. The American Legion could do much more for veterans if it could demand compulsory membership. The Chamber of Commerce in any city could do much more for business if all businessmen had to join and pay dues.

"Unionizing and collective bargaining are premised on the free choice of individuals who work together to join a union of their choice, and to bargain collectively," declared Senator John McClellan of Arkansas in a 1959 Senate debate. "It is not based on compulsion to join a union.

" 'Compulsion' is an ugly word. Decent unionism does not require it.... If unionism is good, if it is sound, if it is just, we can trust in the good faith and the quality of integrity in American workers *voluntarily* to accept it... The workers will seek to unionize. But they ought not be compelled and highjacked to join unions."

What about the contention by labor leaders that "right-to-work" laws weaken unions?

The facts are these: In the 19 states which now have right-to-work laws, union membership has grown faster than in states which do not! During the 1959 Congressional debate on revising Taft-Hartley legislation, the U.S. Chamber of Commerce presented figures showing that during the period 1939-53, trade union membership growth averaged 192.

r cent in right-to-work states, and 187.8 per cent in states
ithout such laws on the books.

Conservative leaders are by no means unanimous in their
pport of right-to-work legislation. In many highly indus-
ialized and unionized states, it is little short of political
icide to do so. But a majority of Conservatives across the
ation agree that the benefits achieved through compulsory
nionism do not justify the loss of individual freedom
volved.

What is the Conservative position on minimum-wage legis-
tion?

Their faith in the free marketplace concept makes it
oubtful that Conservatives will ever support government at-
mpts to establish wage levels. In general, they believe that
arrent Liberal attempts to raise minimum wages and ex-
nd them to more areas of the economy can only result in
reater unemployment, higher prices, and restricted business
xpansion.

Eugene Sydnor, presenting the U.S. Chamber of Com-
erce case against raising the minimum wage, had this to
ay during 1960 Senate hearings:

"When the minimum-wage level is raised, the business-
an has two alternatives to compensate for added labor
osts—

"1. He can attempt to raise prices ...

"2. He can reduce the number of employees.

"Either of these two choices is economically harmful. . . ."

In a 1961 address, Senator Goldwater gave his views on
hat happens when the minimum wage is increased:

"The first ones to be let go when employers begin shoulder-
g increased labor costs without a corresponding boost in
roductivity will be the unskilled, the older workers, and
e very young. These are the workers at the lower fringe
f the wage scale, among whom jobless rates have been the
ighest. I believe much of the trouble these people are
aving today can be traced to previous increases in the
inimum wage. High-sounding attempts to help them

through legislative means has actually been hurting them by cutting down employment opportunities."

The American Farm Bureau Federation position was stated in Senate minimum wage hearings by William Kuhfuss, president of the Illinois Agriculture Association:

"We do not believe that Government regulation of wages (or prices) will ever function as effectively and efficiently as the market mechanism. To the extent that wage legislation interferes with production, to the extent that it discourages individuals from undertaking enterprises they might otherwise have undertaken ... to this extent, minimum wage legislation reduces, rather than increases, the real earning capacity of workers."

Nothing angers the average American more than disclosures of violations of the public trust.

Americans were stung to anger by the recent revelation of unlawful price fixing on the part of electrical equipment manufacturers, just as they had been by disclosures of crimes committed against the public by the giant industrial monopolies of Teddy Roosevelt's day. They were angered by the news, in 1962, that certain companies had been gouging the federal government through "profit pyramiding" in the missile program.

The public ire is aroused just as readily by labor union misdeeds. The dirt dredged up by the McClellan Subcommittee on Labor Rackets shocked all Americans and provided the exciting raw material for Robert Kennedy's best seller *The Enemy Within*.

The national sense of fair play is affronted by union "feather-bedding" practices on the railroads, and by such actions as the New York electricians' strike for a 25-hour week.

When abuses occur on a program affecting national security, the federal government can get most unhappy, too, Senator Karl Mundt told his constituents about one such case in a 1961 newsletter:

"Evidence unfolding before the Senate Subcommittee on Investigations, on which I serve as ranking Republican, con-rms early reports that our missile construction program has ecome a 'gravy train' and a 'loafers' paradise'—at the ex- ense of the nation's taxpayers—for certain individuals whose ersonal greed apparently exceeds their patriotism. . . .

"Perhaps the most shocking . . . abuse revealed is the prac- ce of 'blessing the manifolds.' In this instance, a piece of quipment for a missile is received 'ready to go' from the ctory. However, the plumbers and pipefitters insisted the anifold required cleaning, which involved the complete dis- ssembly, the 'cleaning' procedure, and reassembly of the anifold, resulting in an unnecessary additional cost to the overnment.

"Since the 'cleaning' operation involved the danger of amage or faulty reassembly, the plumbers and pipefitters de- eloped the 'blessing' scheme. When the manifold was re- eived, the workers simply sat around doing nothing for the eriod of time normally involved in taking it apart and put- ng it together again. After several hours, the manifold was iven a 'blessing'—an approval by the union—that the equip- nent was ready for installation in the missile."

A vast majority of union members are honest, hard-work- g people who get as angry at such practices as anybody se. But their protests too seldom result in corrective action. many cases, the McClellan Subcommittee investigation owed, workers who protested too strenuously were expelled om their unions and thereafter found it almost impossible get work.

Moreover, the government seems unable to punish offend- g union leaders with the same prompt effectiveness dis- ayed in the conviction of the electrical equipment price xers.

Fortunately for America, there are many more good unions an bad ones—and many more honest union leaders than acketeers.

But, Conservatives repeatedly point out, the immense ower which now rests in the hands of union leadership ill be a continuing invitation to wrongdoing.

So long as our laws permit labor union leaders to keep

their members in line by threatening loss of their live
hood ... so long as union members can be forced to co
tribute to the election of public officials favored by th
leaders ... so long as national unions can go to the barga
ing table as one industry-wide force pitted against ma
competing corporate employers....

... Then the balance of power will remain heavily
favor of union leadership.

It is not surprising that Conservatives should take t
stands they take in labor relations. In a political philosop
which stresses freedom of action, it is entirely logical th
the freedom of joining—or not joining—a union should
cherished; that the freedom of members to shape uni
policy and criticize their officers should be guaranteed; th
the increasing accumulation of power in the hands of lab
leaders should be looked upon with apprehension.

Today's Conservatives are not anti-labor. But they a
against monopoly power wherever they find it entrenched.

XIII.

■ EDUCATION IS EVERYBODY'S CONCERN

If there is one thing upon which all Americans can agree, it is on the vital role of education in the unfolding drama of the 1960s.

It is education, we agree, which will provide the growing numbers of scientists and technicians we so desperately need to keep America the strongest nation in the world. It is education we count on to provide the informed electorate without which there can be no successful government by the people. It is education which will help provide the buying power to keep industry growing. It is education which will enable our children to deal intelligently with whatever baffling problems the future may bring.

America is as solidly for education as it is for motherhood and against sin.

Why, then, has education aroused such tumult and shouting in recent years?

The central argument is boiling and bubbling around the question of *who is responsible* for providing the education we all agree is absolutely essential.

Quite predictably, the Liberals argue that the education of our children in these crucial times has become such a national concern that we can no longer continue the American tradition of leaving the responsibility entirely to the local school districts and the states. The Liberal solution to the problem of education is the same as the Liberal solution to most other problems: *Federal aid*.

Just as predictably, Conservatives put their trust in solutions formulated and financed on the local level. And they point out that local responsibility for education is more than tradition—it is Constitutional law.

"How can we improve our educational system?" asks

former Vice-President Richard Nixon in his book *The Challenges We Face,* published in 1960. "We hear a great deal about what the Federal government can and should do. There are some who ask: why can't we have far greater Federal responsibility for education at the primary level, the secondary level, and the college level as well?

"In the Soviet Union, this would be the logical and only approach. But one of the matchless strengths of this nation is that our schools have always been primarily a local concern. The individual citizen is responsible, with his neighbor, for the quality and caliber of our total educational system.

"One very important principle for us to bear in mind is that the hallmark of freedom is diversity. We do not want our educational standards established either in Washington or, for that matter, in the state capital, and made absolutely uniform for all of the people and all of the students in the schools. . . .

"We must recognize that diversity in education, as in every other field, is one of the guarantees of freedom."

Nixon advocates a middle-of-the-road approach—Federal aid for school construction, but not for teacher salaries or scholarship grants, as Liberal leaders are demanding.

Most Conservatives take an even firmer stand against federal financing of schools.

Rep. Peter Frelinghuysen, Jr., of New Jersey, speaking for a task force from the House Republican Policy Committee, had this to say about how federal financing of education leads to federal control:

"When we closely examine large Federal programs in highways, urban renewal, agriculture, welfare and similar matters, we find that controls generally tighten as the Federal share increases. Each conflict between Federal and local officials . . . leads to quarrels over the most effective use of funds and almost inevitably is decided by the power of the purse strings held by the Federal Government."

Then Frelinghuysen touched on a point which Conservatives feel cannot be overemphasized:

"Even should Federal aid without Federal control somehow be possible," he said, "the fact that decision making is taken away from parents, communities and legislatures—

since a share of the funds does not depend upon their direct approval and control—in effect is a shifting of effective control. Independence of the educational administration from legislators, boards and the lay public would result, even if Federal control *per se* did not."

That is a foundation stone of the Conservative argument. Even if the Federal Government stays completely out of the business of controlling the schools it helps to finanace, local control of education is weakened by the simple fact that local power of the purse is weakened.

There is another facet of federal assistance that worries Conservatives, and that is the tendency of local school districts to put off needed programs in the hope that the Federal government may soon come in and finance the programs for them.

"Letters are on file with Congressman after Congressman testifying to just what a mere debate on Federal aid proposals has already done to local incentive," Frelinghuysen reported. "School superintendents have recommended defeat of local bond issues and local citizens have testified that their community should defeat increases in local taxation for the simple reason that 'next year the Federal government will pay for our new building, or swimming pool, or additional school buses.' To us, this is a strong warning that Federal aid might well mean a significant weakening of local concern and incentive for public education."

"Nobody—except possibly the most radical of socializers—seems to want federal control of education. The American Education Association says it doesn't want it. Abraham Ribicoff, the New Frontier's first Secretary of Health, Education and Welfare, says he doesn't want it. Even the radical Americans for Democratic Action say they don't want it."

All they want is for the federal government to turn over to the schools a few billion dollars—with no strings attached, they want it made clear—to use as they see fit. Then most of the problems facing American education will disappear like an early morning fog.

The reasoning of federal aid advocates seems naive to most Conservatives. Taxpayers in the 42,000-plus school districts of the nation cannot provide enough money to finance education, say the Liberals. So that money must be provided from an *outside* source—the federal government.

Here again, Liberals exhibit that curious faith in a sort of good fairy in Washington who can come up with any needed sum of money to finance any worthy project. They seem incapable of understanding that federal tax money can come from only one source—*the same citizens who pay taxes in the 42,000 school districts.*

Nothing is gained by calling in the federal government to collect and distribute these extra funds, and much is lost. In the first place, there is the federal handling charge, the money paid federal officials to collect and disperse it. More important, there is the loss in local self-sufficiency and local control of schools.

What is the nature of the problem which federal aid to education is being called upon to solve?

It cannot be denied that there is a problem, although there is much evidence that advocates of federal aid have magnified it far beyond its actual size. There *is* a shortage of classrooms—as any parent whose children attend double sessions can verify. Too many children *are* handicapped by old and inadequate facilities. Teachers' salaries, in general, *are* too low.

But what is the magnitude of the classroom shortage, how many more teachers do we need, how great is the discrepancy in teachers' salaries—and what have the local school districts and the states been doing about it?

First, let us consider the classroom shortage: Between 1954 and 1959, according to figures obtained from the U.S. Office of Education and published in a paper by President Ernest Wilkinson of Brigham Young University, the classroom shortage had *shrunk* from 370,000 (in elementary and secondary schools combined) to 132,400.

A 1961 report released by the Department of Health, Education and Welfare stated that the nation should build 607,600 new classrooms during the decade of the 1960s to erase the classroom deficit, replace obsolete facilities, and provide for anticipated growth in enrollment.

And how well are the local school districts doing in their efforts to meet that goal? In the five-year period of 1956-61, the schoolroom construction pace was just under 70,000 per year—enough to reach the HEW goal and provide nearly 100,000 *excess* classrooms by 1970!

Second, consider the teacher shortage: In the last 30 years, reports Rep. Frelinghuysen, employment in public education has increased by 140 per cent, as compared to 45 per cent in private industry. The number of students per teacher has decreased from 35.6 in 1900 to 24.4 today. In the next ten years, the number of certified teachers is expected to *double*, but the school age population is expected to increase only *20 per cent*.

And third, consider teachers' salaries: In the past five years, teachers' salaries have increased an average of $250 per year. In the past 30 years, teachers' salaries have risen 206 per cent, based on constant dollar value, as compared with 91 per cent for all salary and wage earners and 73 per cent for civilian employees of the federal government.

No one will deny that there is still much room for improvement in the national educational picture. But what amazing strides have been made in recent years!

"Between 1900 and 1956 the total resources committed to education in the United States rose about 3½ times relative to consumer income in dollars, and relative to the gross formation of physical capital in dollars," reported Professor Theodore Schultz of the University of Chicago in a 1961 study.

Even more startling, educational expenditures have increased by *642 per cent* since 1940, while public school enrollment has increased only *57 per cent* during the same period.

In 1930, Americans spent 3.7 per cent of their income on education. By 1950, that figure had risen to 4.1 per cent, and today it is over 6 per cent.

Is there anything in these figures which indicates that local financing of our schools has failed, and that the federal government must now step in?

Conservatives who oppose federal aid to education should understand what is implied in the term, since there has been federal aid of one kind or another since pre-Constitution days

The Survey Ordinance adopted in 1785 reserved one section of every township in the Western Territory for the endowment of schools within that township. The Morrill Act of 1862 granted federal lands to each state for the establishment of today's land grant colleges. The Smith-Hughes Act of 1917 set up federal grants to promote vocational education in public schools.

In more modern times we have had the Lanham Act (1940), authorizing federal aid to local governments in communities swollen by military personnel and defense workers; the GI Bill of Rights (1944), setting up educational benefits for veterans; the National School Lunch Act (1946), giving money and surplus food to schools for lunch programs; PL 874 (1950), authorizing federal payments for schools in areas overburdened ("impacted") by federal installations; and the National Defense Education Act (1958), authorizing $1 billion in grants for improving the teaching of science, mathematics and foreign languages.

But "federal aid to education" today commonly refers to proposals to spend federal money for school construction, teachers' salaries, scholarships and other benefits to schools at all levels.

Such proposals have been made every year since 1945. Federal aid for public school construction came within a whisker of passing Congress in a dramatic 1960 battle, which found both houses approving construction aid and the Senate going even further to add teacher salary funds. But adjournment came before differences in the two versions could be resolved.

Both 1960 party platforms promised federal aid to education—the Democrats pledging federal grants for both construction and salaries, and the Republicans promising only construction aid.

Conservatives are not in agreement as to how much—if any—help the federal government should render. Many oppose any federal aid, of any kind, to any school, at any time. Many others support such long-established programs as vocational education, school lunches and aid to federally-impacted areas. Still others go along with the more recent programs of federal support of scientific research and science teaching.

There was strong Conservative support for the College Academic Facilities Bill, passed by the House in 1962, which provided for loans and grants to build college classrooms. Arizona's Rep. John Rhodes, a consistent Conservative voter, explained his support of the bill in this way: "I supported this bill because it met the criteria I have always demanded of any federal aid legislation—there is a genuine need for the assistance and there is no element of federal control of higher education. . . ."

But nearly all Conservatives agree that there is great danger in today's proposals for multi-billion-dollar federal aid to the nation's elementary and high school districts to pay teachers' salaries and build new classrooms. Not only would such aid impose federal control over public schools—as federal aid does in almost every area—but it is clearly unnecessary.

We have been so busy in recent years discussing the problems and failures of American education that we tend to overlook its great and lasting accomplishments.

Mr. Nixon cites these evidences that American school facilities are more than adequate, and that the schools have been doing a superlative job:

1. Only four other countries—Norway, Sweden, the Netherlands and Japan—share with us the accomplishment of having 99 per cent of their elementary school age children attending school.

2. The percentage of students beyond elementary school age who attend high school and college is higher in America than in any other country.

3. We have more classrooms and other equipment for our student population than any other nation.

4. We have more technically and professionally trained people in our population than any other nation.

5. And we have reduced illiteracy to 3 per cent of the total population—an accomplishment exceeded only by Norway and Sweden.

American teachers are better educated today than ever before. There has never been more public interest in educational problems. Our children are remaining in school for more years—and, in general, learning more—than ever before.

Can we, then, be satisfied with the present status of American education?

No.

Conservatives and Liberals alike agree that Americans can never afford to stop improving educational facilities and, more important, educational quality.

And there is some room for bettering educational quality without additional expense.

There is a growing conviction among Conservatives—and it is shared by many liberals—that our schools can raise educational quality by placing more emphasis on subject matter and less on "social adjustment." Educational quality can be raised, they believe, by requiring that more student time be spent on such tool subjects as English, mathematics, history and basic sciences.

The first duty of the schools is to impart the accumulated wisdom of the race to our children, not to teach them adjustment, declares Dr. Max Rafferty in his new book *Suffer, Little Children.* Too many teachers, he says, with their field trips, group dynamics and emphasis on maturation levels, have picked the meat from the bones of education and replaced it with pablum.

Educational quality could be boosted, too, say many Conservatives, by allowing students to face the challenges of possible failure. In too many schools, students are judged more on effort than on achievement, and virtually all are passed on to the next higher grade at the end of the year. The result is a general leveling and lowering of educational standards.

School should provide training for life, and there is disappointment and failure in life as surely as there is achievement and success. If competition is minimized in school—if children are made to feel that it is more important to be an amiable, average member of the group than to strive for high achievement—we can expect a national drift toward placid mediocrity.

What are the Conservative programs for strengthening American education?

The House Republican Policy Committee task force report

f 1961 contains many of these Conservative proposals.
Among them:

"It is an established and sound principle that the control
nd direction of educational resources in America belongs on
local level. . . .

"The proposals for Federal aid to education now before
Congress would do much, in our judgment, to curtail the
ery factors now promoting a healthy and sound educational
ystem. . . . Controls from Washington would certainly in-
rease, coupled with the void caused by the abandonment
f decision-making powers of parents, communities and
gislatures. . . .

"We suggest that experimentation with so-called progres-
ive education . . . be matched with comparable experimenta-
on with basic, fundamental education. . . .

"We urge our colleagues to exert every effort in influencing
heir constituents . . . to exert leadership in matters relating
o schools—their improvement, their control, their financing
nd their importance. . . .

"Experimentation with educational television, homogeneous
lasses, teaching machines, computer aids in marking, and
ther bookkeeping functions now occupying the time of
eachers, should continue in order to get more education
or our money. . . .

"It is time we begin to consider maximum utilization . . .
f our educational facilities on a more regular basis than 6½
ours per day, 5 days per week, 9 months per year. A 12-
month school year with staggered vacations might well be
nstituted on an experimental basis. . . .

"We would hope that the House Ways and Means Committee would consider the return of a portion of (federal)
evenues to State and local jurisdictions, or the proposals such
s those advocated by Representative Poff to authorize cred-
ts against the Federal income tax for new prospective
State and local taxes imposed for school purposes. . . ."

Local financing, local control, local interest—increased use
f television and other modern aids—better utilization of
xisting school facilities—more emphasis on basic, fundamen-
al education—tax credits for school financing——these are
he Conservative proposals.

American public education is the envy of the rest of the world. The people in our school districts, with support from our state governments, have demonstrated their willingness to take the interest and pay the price to keep American education the best on the face of the earth.

XIV.

■ HOW FREE THE ECONOMY?

In 1961, 2.2 million new workers entered the scramble for jobs in America. By 1970, according to our best estimates, that figure will have climbed to 3 million.

Where will those jobs come from?

No other question of the 1960s is of greater concern to 85 million Americans.

Without a job, a potential producer becomes a drag on his fellow citizens. Without a job, a man ceases to be a free, self-sufficient individual and soon sinks to dependency on private charity or government handouts.

To the Conservative, the prospect of 3 million new recruits being added to the labor force each year is hardly a frightening one. Instead, it presents an exciting challenge. Three million new workers each year can add immeasurably to America's already vast productive capacity, and they can swell the market for an infinite number of new goods and services.

They can, that is, if enough new jobs can be created to absorb the new workers.

How are jobs created?

In our American economic system, they are created when someone has enough nerve and enough faith in the future to invest in new enterprises, or to expand existing ones.

On the average, an investment of more than $20,000 is required to create each new job. And investments of this magnitude are made only when the investor has a reasonable assurance that he can make a fair return on his money.

Jobs are not created by Congressional action, by Presidential decree, or by any other means than private investment in the tools of production—stimulated by the hope of profit.

It is for this reason that every Conservative proposal for improving the already good health of the American economy is based on the need to maintain an economic climate in which new investment—the stuff of which new jobs are made —becomes increasingly attractive.

"If industry and labor are left to take their own course, they will generally be directed to those objects which are most productive, and this in a more certain and direct manner than the wisdom of the most enlightened Legislature could point out."

James Madison, whose wisdom contributed so mightily to the writing of the United States Constitution, said that 170 years ago. Thomas Jefferson added a corollary to the theorem: "Were we directed from Washington when to sow and when to reap, we should soon want bread."

These words of Madison and Jefferson have been guiding Conservatives in their economic outlook ever since.

There is no persuasion like the persuasion of declining demand to make a company cut back on the production of horse collars. There is no government edict which can prod a machinery manufacturer on to a greater output as effectively as the promise of higher profits.

No legislature, nor even the wisest bureaucrat, can regulate production, prices, consumption or any other function of the economy half as efficiently as can the unrestricted functioning of the free market.

Given a chance to try every available brand of soap chips on the market, consumers will soon decide for themselves how much of Brand A should be produced, and they may so reject Brand X that it will be removed from the grocers' shelves. Consumers will legislate—with their purchases—how much oleomargarine should be manufactured, and how much cream should be churned into butter, and all the cajoling of both the oleomargarine and dairy interests can not change the ratio appreciably.

If one producer, or a group of producers, manages to corner the market on a product and then forces up the price, to the detriment of the general public, then the free market ceases to operate and the public may demand that its government pass laws against such monopolies. This the public has done on many occasions, as the anti-trust laws now on the books will attest.

This concept of government as the referee of the economic contest has long been accepted by Conservatives.

"Moderate public regulation of business is the American middle way—the essentially conservative method of avoiding anarchy on the one hand and socialism on the other," wrote Gordon Harrison in *Road to the Right*. "There could be no surer way of creating an irresistable demand for radical socialism than to demonstrate that regulation won't work."

But there is a yawning chasm between the Conservative concept of government as economic referee and the Liberal concept of government as economic planner.

When government planning is attempted on a large scale, as it has in recent decades, artificial criteria are substituted for those of the free market. When price ceilings are established by law at a figure below what consumers are willing to pay, producers may decide not to invest in new plant facilities, or even suspend production altogether. When wages are artificially pegged at a level which makes further production only marginally profitable, investors are more likely to hoard their risk capital than to put it to work in industrial enterprises.

The inevitable result: New plant construction never gets off the drawing boards, obsolete machinery is kept in service longer, research on new products never begins.

And there are fewer jobs.

"It is unquestionably owing to our free economy that we have become the most productive country in the world," said the late Senator Robert Taft in 1949. "We have come where we are because the American still has the right to keep the proceeds of his efforts. . . . The Socialists overlook the tremendous importance of . . . incentive—the fact that most men do not like to work unless there is something to be gained. . . .

"I am opposed to price and wage control, to the prohibition of strikes even if collective bargaining has failed, to allocation controls, and in general to all attempts to substitute government planning for the normal forces of competition."

Liberals often express their inability to understand why Conservatives are so opposed to "planning." We plan our family economics and our individual business operations, they point out. Why, then, should not government plan the nation's economic growth?

Conservatives oppose government planning of the national economy because such planning—in order to have any effectiveness at all—must imply *control* as well. Government cannot plan the production of steel, or cotton, or automobiles without forcing the producers to conform to the production goals it arbitrarily establishes. Government cannot plan a wage structure without forcing employers to adhere to it. Moreover, as Madison so wisely foresaw, no government can plan for optimum production and consumption nearly as well as can producers and consumers operating in an essentially free market.

And even if a government *could* regulate as effectively as does the free market, the freedom of the people must be decreased as the degree of government planning increases.

The free market is not always kind. The town ice plant closes down and hundreds of lifelong employees are forced to seek new jobs and train for new skills. The man who invests his savings in the manufacture of 3-D theater glasses finds himself with a million unsalable glasses and no savings.

But the government is not making any long-term contribution to the victims of technological change by enforcing minimum wages in ice plants or subsidizing the continued manufacture of 3-D glasses. Eventually, those involved will be forced to obey the natural laws of supply and demand. And in the meantime, the financial losses incurred by government must be made up by more successful producers.

"It is a revealing fact that few planners are content to say that central planning is desirable," declared Peter Hayek in his book *Road to Serfdom.* "Most of them affirm that we can no longer choose, but are compelled by circumstances beyond our control to substitute planning for competition. The myth is deliberately cultivated that we are embarking on the new course, not out of free will, but because competition is spontaneously eliminated by technological changes which we can neither reverse nor should wish to prevent. . . . This argument is devoid of foundation."

Conservatives reject the government-planned economy for two reasons:

1. It restricts individual freedom, and
2. It just doesn't work.

Nowhere has the folly of government planning been more evident than in the sad story of 30 years of farm controls.

"Our trouble commenced when we first accepted the notion that government intervention—subsidies, controls, concessions, etc. —could be substituted for the creative strength of a free people," Senator Goldwater told Texas cattlemen at a 1960 dinner. "We forgot momentarily that liberty is indivisible. We cannot have liberty in any realm of our personal activities unless we are willing to accept liberty in all areas. We cannot have economic freedom and political dictation, nor can we have political freedom and economic dictation. . . .

"Let me emphasize here and now that the farmers are the victims, not the creators, of our disastrous farm policy. . . . The total 'realized cost' . . . from 1932 to 1959 has been $17,753,000,000. Farm surpluses today are 3½ times as large as they were at the beginning of 1953. Carrying charges, transportation, interest and the cost of storage amount to more than one billion dollars a year. . . .

"The tragic thing about all of these programs of big government intervention is that they invariably produce waste and create a dependent society."

America's farmers time and time again have made the Washington planners look ridiculous by coaxing more and more production out of fewer and fewer acres.

U.S. News and World Report, commenting Nov. 13, 1961, on the disappointing results of the New Frontier's experimental feed grains program, had this to say:

"Once more, Washington is learning a lesson about farmers.

"The story: Government, in a new program, paid farmers to cut acres planted to feed grains. Price supports were raised.

"Idea was to reduce output by nearly a billion bushels.

"Actual cut: only half that much. Taxpayers are out 880 million dollars, and output still exceeds the country's needs . . .

"It's the same kind of ride that farmers gave Henry Wallace back in 1933. They have been repeating the performance for planners ever since. . . ."

Arizona cotton farmers, Kansas wheat farmers, Illinois corn farmers—all respond to restrictions in the same way. They produce more crops on fewer acres in a valiant effort to keep their income from further reduction. As a result, surpluses are piled higher, and the nation pays the subsidy bill.

"For God's sake, let the Russians get to the moon first," a constituent wrote Rep. Durward G. Hall of Missouri recently. "If we get there, we might learn how to grow wheat there, and then we *would* be in trouble."

Conservatives believe the answer to the nation's farm problem is a gradual withdrawal from agricultural acreage limitations and federal subsidies. The American farmer, they are convinced, can work out his problems—individually and cooperatively—once the working of the free market is substituted for the experimentation of government planners.

Then all American taxpayers, farmers included, would be relieved of most of the cost for farm programs—a cost which hit $5.1 billion in fiscal 1961, rose to $6.2 billion in fiscal 1962, and shows every sign of climbing still higher in the future.

Senator Mundt was steaming on that afternoon of June 7, 1961, and it wasn't because of the Washington weather.

Less than an hour before, the Senate had voted for federal operation of a steamship line between Washington state and Alaska. The cost to taxpayers: $375,000.

"Under the Eisenhower Administration, we made real progress in getting the government out of operations which really were the function of private enterprise," he declared. "We were able to 'de-socialize' a large number of government-owned and operated competitive enterprises. But today we have gone backward a huge step in approving a $375,000 appropriation to purchase new facilities to operate this government-owned shipping line."

It was another skirmish—and a losing one for Conservatives —in the continuing battle over federal competition with private business.

In a March, 1962, resolution proposing a Senate investigaion of such competition, Senator Tower of Texas listed some major examples of federal participation in business and industry:

1. The Postal Savings System, competing with commercial savings institutions.
2. The Military Air Transport Service, operating flights on routes served by commercial airlines.
3. The Alaska Communications System, still government owned and operated despite the availability of private buyers.
4. The Tennessee Valley Authority, which sells $20 million worth of fertilizer annually—at below cost.
5. The Navy, which is assigning 75 per cent of its repair and conversion on naval vessels to its own shipyards despite its admission that costs are as much as 15 per cent higher than in private yards.
6. Federal power agencies, generating 112,305,000 kilowatt-hours of electrical energy in 1960—nearly three times as much as in 1950.
7. The Defense Department, which owns and operates more than 100 local telephone systems. The Department would rather sell them to private buyers, but Congressional restrictions make such sales difficult.

"There are many ways to confiscate private property or replace it with government-run operations," said Senator Tower in presenting his resolution. "Inequitable and excessive taxation is one way; attempts to cure the threat of bankruptcy by more spending is another. Stringent government controls are another. Government ownership is the most direct way, and it is this that should be examined and corrected by Congress as soon as possible."

Little by little, the federal government has crept into almost every kind of business. Many compete directly with private enterprise. Many others are not in direct competition, but their functions could be performed more economically by privately-owned taxpaying firms.

Conservatives argue that one of the best and easiest ways to boost the nation's economy would be to get the federal government out of private business as soon as possible. The benefits would be many and immediate: Reduction of costs to taxpayers ... creation of new business opportunities and new jobs ... and replacement of tax *draining* enterprises with tax *producing* ones.

Conservatives believe there are still other steps government must take—besides getting out of economic planning activity and out of competition with private enterprise—to give the economy maximum opportunity to grow.

One is to adopt more realistic allowances for the obsolescence of industrial machinery.

"Under the conditions of growth in our dynamic economy today, machines become rapidly obsolescent," said the 1961 report of the House Republican Policy Committee. "*One-third* of our industrial plant is in this condition today. Depreciation allowances lag $4 to $6 billion annually behind replacement needs.

"Great Britain allows over 40 per cent depreciation on new machinery in the year of acquisition. Germany allows a write off of 25 per cent the first year and about 58 per cent of cost in the first three years. France allows 30 per cent for ordinary machinery, with the remaining percentage depreciable at 15 per cent of original cost and written off in less than five more years. ...

"We recommend more adequate and sensible depreciation allowances to stimulate investment in plant and equipment, and eventually, in ultimate increased employment opportunities."

Government has other responsibilities in the promotion of the nation's economic growth: encouragement of research ... assembling and dissemination of business statistics ... support in developing foreign markets ... encouragement of the retraining of workers idled because their skills have become obsolete or surplus.

And, even more important, in reducing taxes—corporate, excise and personal income taxes.

"The small loss of revenue caused by some reduction of these (tax) rates would inevitably be offset by new investment and business expansion," explains former Vice-President Nixon. "The charge will inevitably be made that such eforms will benefit business and not the people. . . . (But) et us understand once and for all that 'business' *is* the people.' The people own it. . . . They depend on business for rogress, for opportunity, for their mutual well-being, and or the development and production of the military equipnent which shields the nation against aggressions."

Whatever government can do to encourage the growth of he nation's privately-owned productive capacity will help not nly business, but labor, agriculture, the professions—in short, ll Americans.

Finally, what can business do for *itself*?

Conservatives traditionally have been too ready to blame overnment interference and taxation for our economic ills, nd too eager to point to organized labor's demands as the ole cause of spiraling costs.

But would the government restrictions of the Teddy Roosevelt era have been necessary had business been more eady to consider the public welfare? Would the regulation f the New Deal have come about if business had been more rudent and less greedy in the Harding and Coolidge prosperity days? Would Big Labor enjoy such sweeping powers oday if industry had been more willing to improve working onditions and wage scales *on its own,* instead of waiting ntil it was forced to do so?

It is impossible to calculate the loss in public confidence which results from a single price-fixing or profit-gouging scandal. And even the public reaction against the Administraion's retaliatory tactics did not entirely erase the ill will enerated by the incredibly bad timing of the 1962 steel price ike.

"The reservoir of good will toward business is great, but ot inexhaustible," wrote Gordon Harrison. "It can endure so ong as it remains possible to reconcile capitalist freedom vith justice and stability."

So it seems clear that business, which long ago forsook its attitude of "the public be damned" and took its place as a esponsible partner in the building of a greater American

economy, must adopt continuing self-regulation as a necessar
condition for self-preservation.

Moreover, business can help its own cause by stepping up
its fight against waste and instituting even greater economie
in production and distribution—by daring to price for eve
greater volume sales with low unit profits—and by investing even greater portions of its income in research and product development.

The men who direct the destinies of business and industry
in America's free enterprise economy hold a public trust ne
less sacred than that which has been bestowed on the hold
ers of the highest elective offices of the nation.

On their vigor, and imagination, and integrity depend
in ever-increasing measure, the economic prosperity of the
1960s, and perhaps the freedom of all Americans for many
decades to come.

XV.

■ THE THORNY QUESTION OF CIVIL RIGHTS

A screaming, rock-throwing mob closes in on a University of Mississippi dormitory, vowing to "get that nigger" who has dared to seek admission.

A Jewish doctor and his wife discover that every hotel in New England resort has suddenly filled up and not a room available.

A Detroit Negro finds he is barred from a multitude of jobs which eventually go to white workers not as well-qualified as he.

An engineer of Japanese descent finds it all but impossible to buy a home in some sections of a California city.

A Negro professor, holder of the Ph.D. degree, finds he is not allowed to vote in an Alabama town on grounds of "illiteracy."

Such violations of the American ideal of equality of opportunity and equal justice under law infuriate most Americans—Conservatives and Liberals alike.

There is no more explosive problem before Americans today than that of racial and religious discrimination. No problem so viciously divides and degrades us. And no other problem so greatly weakens our efforts to win the vast non-white and non-Christian populations of the world to our point of view.

Most of our problems of racial and religious discrimination are popularly lumped together as violations of "civil rights." This designation is not entirely accurate, however, as many Conservative spokesmen have pointed out. Actually, a "civil" right is one which is guaranteed by a valid law. There are no federal statutes, for example, which make it mandatory for a hotel to accept all who seek accommodations, or which require a school district to racially integrate its schools.

157

A large majority of Americans recognize the right to use public accommodations and public schools as a *human* right, but it is not in most states a *civil* right. The right to vote, on the other hand, may not be denied because of race, color or previous servitude, and this is a civil right guaranteed by the Constitution.

Call them what you will, the rights of opportunity, justice and human dignity are given vocal support by most Americans. The tragedy is that there is too often a gulf between the rights we proclaim and the rights we uphold in practice.

Americans in other sections of the nation cherish the notion that the race problem is the exclusive property of the South. But such is not the case.

Negro populations in almost every metropolitan center are growing faster than are white populations. Washington, D.C., is now three-fourths Negro. Cleveland, Chicago, New York, Detroit, St. Louis and many other cities have skyrocketing Negro populations.

And their racial tensions tend to mount as the Negro exodus from the South continues.

The many and thorny aspects of the race relations problem lie at the heart of the question of civil rights. The problems are becoming increasingly national in nature, and they must be solved. But by whom? And by what means?

Here again, there are marked differences in the Liberal and the Conservative approach.

"Let us begin by stressing that no matter how convinced a people may be of the wrongness of an existing situation, it does not follow that the people should be prepared to resort to whatever means may be necessary to attempt to make that situation right," wrote William F. Buckley, Jr., in a November 11, 1961, *Saturday Review* article opposing federally-enforced desegregation.

"That may sound obvious—the end does not justify any means; but when we examine some of the drastic proposals that are being put forward with the end of securing the rights of the Negro . . . the time has come to reiterate the obvious. . . .

"*Should* we resort to convulsive measures that do violence to the traditions of our system in order to remove the forms of segregation in the South? If the results were predictably and unambiguously successful, the case might be made persuasively. If a clean stroke through the tissue of American mores could reach through to the cancer, forever to extirpate it, then one might say, in due gravity: let us operate. But when the results are thus ambiguous? Use the federal power to slash through the warp and woof of society in pursuit of a social ideal which was never realized even under the clement circumstances of a Chicago or a New York or Philadelphia?

"I say no. A conservative is seldom disposed to use the Federal Government as the sword of social justice, for the word is generally two-edged. . . ."

Here Buckley has stated two of the basic Conservative positions on race relations: First, that the federal government is not the proper agency of solution and has no legal right to intervene in the race problems of the states, and second, that there is no assurance that such intervention would solve those problems.

"Once before, in Prohibition, the United States experimented with sociology," pointed out Thomas Waring, editor of the *Charleston* (S.C.) *News and Courier*, in a 1960 civil rights hearing reported by *Congressional Digest*. "Prohibition was a failure. It brought on bootlegging and a crime wave. Eventually, the people came to their senses. They repealed Prohibition. At least it had the authority of a lawful Constitutional amendment. This time the experiment (with desegregated schools) is with the lives of children—on the basis of court decrees."

Waring was expressing the generally-held southern view. Representative Clare Hoffman of Michigan, in a July 19, 1956, speech in the House of Representatives, spoke for many northern Conservatives when he declared: "We have ample laws protecting our citizens and others who reside with us. If the civil rights of any appreciable number of our people are disregarded, it is because those charged with the enforcement of our present laws either do not wish to enforce them, or their efforts to implement the enforcement are not supported by the people."

Conservatives, in general, do not believe that government action—either through court decrees or by the passage of laws—can deal effectively with so deeply-rooted or so emotionally-based a problem as race relations.

Another northern Congressman, Representative Noah Mason of Illinois, attempted to explain this Conservative viewpoint in a 1957 statement on the House floor: "Habits, customs and obligations are much more effective than any civil rights program implemented by federal laws. Laws are not particularly efficient. Custom is much more effective than any law because it polices itself. A law has little chance of being enforced if it does not have the approval and support of a majority of the people. . . .

"Our times call for patience, for moderation, for gradual *evolution*—not for *revolution* by Federal law or Supreme Court fiat."

This is the generally-held Conservative view. No law can be enforced effectively where there is massive public resistance to it—except by massive force. And when troops and bayonets are employed to bring about social justice, such grudging gains in social justice as may result are more than cancelled out by the losses of freedom to the whole people.

Liberals, generally speaking, are convinced that federal intervention is the only effective solution to the problem of race relations. There has been so little progress in establishing the Negro as a first-class citizen, they say, that only the most drastic remedies will suffice.

There is ample evidence, however, that no other minority racial group in all history has made so much progress as has the American Negro in the past nine decades. It must be remembered that less than 100 years ago Negroes were slaves —creatures without any legal rights, bought and sold and worked like animals.

Today many of them are scientists, high-ranking military officers, judges, artists, professors, surgeons, government officials. The pace of their progress—in large part because of lack of opportunity—is still too slow to suit most of their llow Americans. As a group, they still lag far behind whites both material and intellectual achievement.

But they are gaining steadily, both in achievement and in cceptance by the white citizenry.

"How far will they go on to advance?" asks Buckley. "To he point where social separation will vanish?

"I do not know, but I hope that circumstance will usher that day, and that when the Negroes have finally realized heir long dream of attaining to the status of the white man, he white man will still be free; and that depends, in part, on he moderation of those whose inclination it is to build a uper-state that will give them Instant Integration."

One encouraging trend of the '60s is the increasing murmur f moderation in the South, which may be heard even above he bitter clamor of racial extremists against galling federal in-rvention.

The *Knoxville* (Tenn.) *News Sentinel* editorialized in 1960: It must be generally realized that the repression of Negro citi-ens won't be tolerated indefinitely—and that remedies en-orced by the national will are bound to be more distasteful han measures instituted through compromise."

And the *Charlotte* (N.C.) *Observer*, commenting on sou-hern filibuster tactics to oppose civil rights legislation, said: Here is a fight of words against time, of men against inevita-ility. . . ."

"We recognize that integration is coming," said a thought-ul young Nashville businessman recently, "and we are doing ur best to make it come peacefully and without bitterness. What we resent is having outsiders coming in and cramming ntegration down our throats. This kind of thing won't speed in-egration—it will delay it."

Gradual progress—that is the Conservative way, and it is erhaps the only way a lasting solution to the race problem nay be achieved.

Those who are in a hurry, who want to use federal force o correct the abuses which exist, fail to recognize what im-ressive gains have been, and are being, made.

Although elementary school integration is proceeding at a snail's pace in some highly-publicized areas, it is progressing quietly and rapidly in many others. Negroes are now ac-

cepted at many southern colleges and universities which
would have spurned them a decade ago. Except where mili
tant efforts to force the issue have fanned the fires of hate
mingling of the races is proceeding in public places. And in
creasing numbers of Negroes are being elected to public of
fice.

Given a chance to work out their problems without out
side interference, many southern communities are doing so ef
fectively. Even in some areas which northerners have long
considered incorrigible, attitudes are changing.

It came as a pleasant shock to many *Time* subscribers
outside the South to read in the May 11, 1962, issue that
longtime Alabama Governor "Kissin' Jim" Folsom—at
tempting a political comeback—had told audiences, "The
Civil War is over! Let us join the people together again. Let
us furnish leadership for our colored people. . . . Last year we
turned our bad face to the world. They took pictures of
mobs running around the streets of Birmingham. They was
taking people out at night, floggin' 'em and mutilatin' and
castratin'. Let us have peace in the valley."

While Conservatives view the problems of race relations—
of racial mingling in restaurants and busses and schools, for
example—as a problem to be solved by the people con
cerned, they are much more willing to let the federal govern
ment intervene to insure that all citizens are granted the
Constitutionally-guaranteed right to vote.

The right to vote is not merely a social privilege—it is a
precious civil right. Wherever it can be shown that any citi
zen is being deprived of his franchise because of his color,
Conservatives are generally agreed that the federal govern
ment has a responsibility to see that justice is done.

And there is solid evidence that in some areas of the United
States—not all of them in the South—Negroes are being de
prived of the vote.

On March 15, 1960, reported *U.S. News and World Re
port,* a spokesman for the U.S. Civil Rights Commission said
that 436 complaints regarding suppression of voting had been
filed with the commission since its establishment in 1957.

lost were from the South, but, surprisingly, the fourth largest total—47—came from California.

The record of Negro voting in the South, as reported in a U.S. News study in 1960, has both bright and dismal aspects. On the bright side, Tennessee reported to 62.7 per cent of voting-age Negroes had voted, and Texas Negroes had an even better voting record than whites—43.6 per cent as against 43.5 per cent. On the other hand, Mississippi's white voting record was listed as "not available," but the Mississippi Negro voting record was the South's worst—only 5.2 per cent of voting-age Negro citizens. And, while 62.5 per cent of Alabama's eligible white citizens voted, only 15.5 per cent of the Negroes did so.

Part of the blame for the poor Negro voting percentage in Mississippi and Alabama may be laid to Negro apathy. But only the most naive could fail to suspect coercion of Negro voters in such a situation.

It can hardly be pure chance that in 16 southern counties where Negroes outnumber whites, *not a single Negro vote was cast*. Or that in 49 other counties where Negroes constitute a majority, less than 5 per cent of the vote was cast by Negroes.

It was just such evidence that prompted passage of the 1960 Civil Rights Act, which included the "voting referee" principle proposed in the Senate by Sen. Dirksen of Illinois and in the House by Rep. William McCulloch of Ohio.

The Dirksen proposal contained these elements:

1. When a voter complains to the U.S. Attorney General that he has been denied the right to vote, the Attorney General may request a federal court to determine whether a "pattern of discrimination" exists. If the court so rules, a federal judge is appointed as a voting referee and the complainant is granted an interview.

2. Once the "pattern of discrimination" is determined, any other petitioner of the same race or group may seek, through a referee, a certificate qualifying him to vote.

3. The Justice Department then sends a copy of the referee's report to the state attorney general or to voting officials, along with an order to show cause why the complainant should

be denied the right to vote. The state can then contest the
claim and submit evidence, if desired.

4. If the claim is settled in favor of the complainant, he
may then take his federal certificate to a voting registrar,
register, and vote. Disobedience of the federal order would
subject the offending voting official to contempt action.

Conservatives and Liberals alike can support such efforts
to guarantee the Constitutional rights of all citizens.

But the problem of school integration—which has been
the source of the nation's most highly-publicized race trou-
bles in recent years—is something else again.

In the first place, Conservatives jealously guard the Constitutional right of the states to plan, finance and supervise
their own educational programs. They are wary of any federal attempt to control education.

Most Conservative spokesmen believe that public schools
should be opened to students of all races, colors and creeds.
But they are unwilling to impose their beliefs on the citizens
of states with a different pattern of education.

"It so happens that I am in agreement with the objectives
of the Supreme Court as stated in the (1954) *Brown* decision
(in favor of school intergration)," says Senator Goldwater. "I
believe that it is both wise and just for Negro children to
attend the same schools as whites, and that to deny them
this opportunity carries with it strong implications of infe-
riority. I am not prepared, however, to impose that judgment
of mine on the people of Mississippi or South Carolina, or
to tell them what methods should be adopted and what pace
should be kept in striving toward that goal. . . . Social and cultural change, however desirable, should not be effected by
the engines of national power."

In the second place, Conservatives feel that, even if federal
action were advisable, mandatory school integration would
have to come about through a Constitutional amendment. A
ruling by the Supreme Court, particularly against a background of 90 years of judicial acceptance of segregated
schools, does not bear sufficient weight to overturn the intent

of the 14th Amendment and the doctrine of self-determination of the individual states.

"The Supreme Court justices expressly acknowledged that they were not being guided by the intentions of the (14th) amendment's authors," Senator Goldwater points out. " 'In approaching this problem,' Chief Justice Warren said, 'we cannot turn the clock back to 1868 when the amendment was adopted. . . . We must consider public education in the light of its full development and its present place in American life throughout the nation.' In effect, the Court said that what matters is not the ideas of the men who wrote the Constitution, but the *Court's* ideas."

Senator Strom Thurmond, who agrees neither with the Supreme Court's intent nor its method, told a Senate subcommittee in 1959 that the Court's school integration decisions "ignore the existence of the 10th Amendment to the Constitution, the doctrine of *stare decisis,* and the wisdom of all previous courts. They are based solely on erroneous sociological theories rather than law. . . ."

It may be considered safe to say that the Supreme Court's integration decisions have not been popular with Conservatives, in or outside the South, whether they be for or against school integration.

The problem of school integration is fast becoming one affecting northern cities as well as the South. As Negroes flock to the major metropolitan centers, an explosive situation is building up.

Dr. James Bryant Conant, former Harvard University president and one of the nation's foremost authorities on the problems of American public schools, expressed his concern about this "social dynamite" in his 1961 book, *Slums and Suburbs.*

Forced integration of schools is not the road to the easing of racial tensions, he says.

"It is my belief that satisfactory education can be provided in an all-Negro school through the expenditure of more money for needed staff and facilities," wrote Dr. Conant. ". . . To assume that the schooling of Negroes can be satisfactory only if in each schoolroom there are present some white children is to take an extremely defeatist view of Negro education in the large cities."

After stating his reasons for opposing current proposals to shuttle school children around a city to insure racial mixing of schools, Dr. Conant offered what he considered a better solution. "I think it would be far better," he wrote, "for those who are agitating for deliberate mixing of children to accept *de facto* segregated schools as a consequence of a present housing situation and to work for the improvement of slum schools, whether Negro or white."

To integrate or not to integrate?

Conservatives believe that the racial tensions which have been built up by forced integration in both South and North have more than cancelled out the questionable benefits of such governmental experiments in social progress. If communities, cities and states are allowed to solve their school integration problems themselves—with the assurance that there shall be free expression for citizens of all races at the ballot box—those problems will be solved with the least possible bitterness and strife.

If federal enforcement is not the answer to the problem of assuring full social justice to all—except where the Constitutional rights of citizens are being violated—what, then, do Conservatives propose?

First, that the federal government remove the threat of coercion which has stiffened the backs of so many people in the South and in some other sections where racial tensions exist. The federal government should then continue the elimination of racial discrimination in its own activities, as it has in the banning of Jim Crow from the military services and in the hiring of civilian government employees.

Second, that private business and the labor unions continue to move toward the eradication of racial discrimination in employment and advancement opportunities.

Third, that white citizens in all parts of the nation substitute the rule of brotherhood and justice for that of unreasoning fear and hatred of racial and religious minority groups, to whatever degree that fear and hatred may exist.

Fourth, that members of racial minority groups—and especially Negroes, since they are most numerous and most subject to discrimination—redouble their efforts to earn the respect they so earnestly seek.

And, finally, that all Americans, white and non-white, Christian and non-Christian, recognize that *patience* is the most important ingredient of all in the building of an America where justice and truly equal opportunity will at last prevail.

America has taken giant strides toward the ideal of universal brotherhood in the past century. She will continue to do so, although progress can be impeded by impatience and a resort to force.

That ideal will not be realized in a day, or in a decade. But if enough Americans pursue it—with enough understanding and forebearance—it will one day surely come.

XVI.

■ THE CONSTITUTION: MORE THAN A HANDBOOK

Why all this Conservative reverence for the Constitution?

In every chapter of this book, Conservative spokesmen have cited it, based arguments on it, decried violations of it.

Isn't it possible, by glossing over a Constitutional article here and ignoring a provision there, to take occasional shortcuts to the solutions of problems which plague us in the 1960s?

Many Liberals seem to think so.

"The Constitution is a grand old document," you may hear them say. "The men who framed it did a wonderful job for their time in history, and it has weathered well, too. But it is not entirely adequate for 20th Century America, and the amendment procedure is too cumbersome to keep up with our fast-moving times. If our people can be served best by circumventing it, then let us circumvent it. After all, *people* and their needs are of more vital concern than any document."

Any conservative citizen who fails to see the fallacy and the inherent danger in such arguments has not delved deeply enough into his political philosophy, or into the foundations of republican government.

For America was founded—as all enduring republics have been founded—on constitutional law.

Administrations come and go. Legislatures are transient. Today's court ruling may be overturned by next year's justices. But the basic document on which all of our government and guarantees of freedom are founded must be kept inviolate if we are to live under the rule of law, and not of men. If changing times should make any portion of the basic document oppressive, then we may amend it—as we have

168

done 23 times in our history. But if the advocates of change cannot muster the support necessary to amend it, then, in all probability, the advocated change is not sufficiently sound.

"Our Federal Constitution was based on the conception that the safeguard of free men rested upon explicit law; and that the law should spring from the expressed will of the majority of the people themselves," wrote Herbert Hoover in *The Challenge to Liberty*.

"The unique feature of its framework was the independence of the *executive, legislative,* and *judicial* powers, the checks and balances between State and Federal authority which should guarantee and sustain those rights and liberties 'to the end that it may be a government of laws and not of men!'

"They set up machinery for its amendment that would require time to stop, look and listen in order that transient emotions might cool, in the expectation that, recalling its transcendent purpose, the people should be slow to abrogate their liberties."

There is nothing divine or supernatural about the American Constitution. It was not emblazoned by heavenly fire on tablets of stone. But it *was* fashioned by wise and free men who were willing to surrender a portion of their individual liberty for the greater good of the nation, and it has been maintained in that same spirit by succeeding generations for nearly 200 years.

The Constitution may, at times, seem to impede our progress toward the very goals for which it was established. Its provision for the presidential veto has on occasion frustrated the will of majorities as expressed through Congressional representatives of the people. Its provision for judicial review has many times led to the invalidation of programs favored by the Executive, Congress and the state legislatures.

But its inestimable worth lies in its maintaining of government based on *law* instead of the transient desires of the *men* who may be in power at a given moment.

And it is the rule of law which will insure that the best possible action is taken on behalf of *people*—while at the same time guaranteeing that their freedoms will never be usurped by a ruling elite.

The American Constitution was written and adopted in 1787 by men who had lived under tyranny, who had learned the lessons of history, and who were determined to establish a system of restraints on the accumulation of power in any single authority.

They knew that any unrestrained authority, no matter how benevolent, soon grows in the direction of absolute rule. So they enumerated those powers which were to be granted to the central government and then reserved all others for the states and the people.

They went further.

They divided the powers of the central government and allocated them to three branches of that government: The *Executive,* the *Legislative* and the *Judicial.* Finally, they set up safeguards—checks and balances—to insure that no branch would encroach on the powers intended for either of the others; and then they tied up the whole package with a tortuous amendment procedure.

Had it not been for those safeguards, it is probable that a strong and popular President long ago would have so dominated the government that Congress would have become nothing more than a rubber stamp, and the Supreme Court a body devoted to legal detail. Likewise, Congress might have assumed so much power that the President would be reduced to the status of a figurehead. Though it is less likely, the Supreme Court might have become dominant had it been permitted to take over the role of lawmaker or administrator.

With any one of the three in a dominant position, the freedom of the people soon would have vanished, and the Constitution itself would eventually have been discarded as a lifeless and useless relic.

John C. Calhoun, who battled throughout his public life against any overstepping of Constitutional boundaries, expressed his appreciation for the wisdom of the Constitutional authors in these words:

"The constitution of a government should be moulded so that the possibility of abuse would be reduced to a minimum. A government provided with appropriate checks was constitutional government. ... Such an organism, then, as will furnish the means by which resistance may be systematically and peaceably made, on the part of the ruled, to oppression and abuse of power on the part of the rulers, is the first and indispensable step in the forming of a constitutional government."

Conservatives today battle incessantly for the safeguarding of Constitutional dispersions of power. They resist today's tendency of federal government to move into the areas of action reserved to the states. They oppose the Executive's attempts to take over any of the Congressional prerogatives in the setting of tax rates. They express concern over the Supreme Court's assumption of both legislative and executive functions in the area of school integration.

Standing up for Constitutional restrictions can be a risky business. It is almost sure to get one labeled a "narrow-minded legalist," or worse. But someone must do it, if the vitality of the Constitution is to be maintained for our generation and those to come.

The kind of Constitutional abuse which Conservative spokesmen cite most often is that of Executive encroachment on the powers reserved to the Legislative branch of government.

Not only do Conservatives seek to curb the Presidential appetite for power, but also the empire-building tendencies of the myriad bureaus and commissions which are a part of the Executive branch of modern American government. Conservatives recognize that the complexity of today's society, and the necessity for regulating more segments of it than ever before, have made such Executive agencies a permanent and necessary part of federal government. But they also recognize the dangers inherent in such agencies, which are not directly responsible to the people.

Senator Robert A. Taft seldom let a week go by without sounding a warning to Congress to be vigilant in resisting the pressures of the mushrooming bureaucracy against the walls of Constitutional restraint.

"The only reason we have any real liberty left in the United States is the independence shown by Congress during the past 14 years," Taft told a Springfield, Ohio, audience on September 17, 1952. "There isn't any doubt in my mind that we have represented the attitude of the people of this country against a government-planned economy, power and bureaucracy."

Senator Taft berated President Truman for his intervention in labor disputes, for encroaching on the Congressional prerogative of sending the nation into war, for usurping the treaty-making responsibility of Congress, and for many other excursions into areas Taft considered out of bounds for Presidential action.

Even before President Franklin Delano Roosevelt had branched out into court-packing or secret treaty negotiations, Conservatives were screaming about his fast and loose treatment of the Constitution. It was his domination of Congress —a relationship which for a time found him sending bills to Capitol Hill in the morning and getting them back for signature by afternoon—that prompted former President Hoover to write:

"If we examine the fate of wrecked republics all over the world, we shall find first a weakening of the legislative arm. Herein lay the decay of Continental European Liberalism. . . . It is in the Legislative Halls that Liberty commits suicide, although legislative bodies usually succeed in maintaining their forms. For 200 years the Roman Senate continued as a scene of social distinction and noisy prattle after it had surrendered its responsibilities and the Roman state had become a tyranny. . . .

"In place of the hard-won legislative control, we now have the curious idea that the Executive must protect the people from legislative endeavors to please group and sectional interests by huge and wasteful expenditures. . . .

"Bills giving unprecedented powers to the Executive were drafted outside the Halls of Congress, presented and enacted with scarcely any debate and no opportunity for public opinion to express itself."

Throughout American history, Conservatives have been more willing to trust Congress than the President, or even the Supreme Court. This is understandable in the light of the Conservative principle of power diffusion. It is much more difficult to put together a workable tyranny in an elective body composed of 437 Representatives and 100 Senators than it is in a nine-man appointive Court of a single President.

In this regard, it is interesting to note that most of the "strong" Presidents have been of Liberal tendency and most of the "weak" ones have been more Conservatively inclined. To note this is not to condemn Conservative leadership. For the Presidents which history records as "strong" were, for the most part, those who first wielded their legitimate power effectively and then reached beyond their Constitutional confines to encroach on the powers of the other two branches. Most of the Conservative Presidents have resisted the temptation to assume powers not Constitutionally granted to the Executive, and thus have not dominated the governmental scene.

In these days of Conservative concern over the growing powers being exercised by the Supreme Court, it may be hard to remember that only a few years ago there was widespread worry that the Court was being shunted into the background.

In his 1949 book, *The American Political Mind*, Francis G. Wilson pointed out that "the Supreme Court virtually ceased after 1937 to stand as a censor of Federal legislation, and from the end of 1936 to 1946, no act of Congress was declared unconstitutional."

That same year, Senator Taft decried attempts to weaken the Court's place in the government trinity, declaring:

"Those who would destroy freedom in any country make the courts a tool of the government, as they are in Russia. Modern totalitarian government cannot admit the right of any court to balk its policies. . . . We must oppose the powerful forces that today are still attempting to take from the courts the power to interpret the Constitution."

The Supreme Court did not accept a place in the back seat for long.

During the decade of the 1950s it asserted itself so energetically that, in the minds of many Conservatives, it overstepped its Constitutional authority.

Senator Sam J. Ervin of North Carolina—a former North Carolina Supreme Court justice—declared in a May 11, 1959, *U.S. News and World Report* article that the U.S. Supreme Court has in reality been amending the Constitution under the guise of interpreting it.

"The truth is that on many occasions during recent years the Supreme Court has usurped and exercised the power of the Congress and the States to amend the Constitution while professing to interpret it," he said.

"If the thesis that a majority of members of the Supreme Court have the rightful power to change the meaning of the Constitution under the guise of interpreting it every time a sitting justice wavers in mind or a newly-appointed Justice ascends the bench should find permanent acceptance, the Constitution would become, to all practical intents and purposes, an uncertain and unstable document of no beneficial value to the country."

Today the Supreme Court is wielding its power with an energy not surpassed in this century. The March 26, 1962, Court decision which established federal authority over reapportionment of Congressional districts within the States is one of several recent decisions affecting all Americans. It provoked some Conservative ire, but it prompted approving comment, too. The Republican Party publication *Battle Line* said that "the result of the Supreme Court decision will be the correction of gross injustices of representation which should have been removed by State legislatures without prodding by the judiciary."

Whether or not the Court in its new self-assertion will weaken the Constitution or give it new life remains to be seen. But nearly 200 years of American history has established the Court as an essentially Conservative force—a force which has protected the nation from radical legislation and Executive action. Moreover, it has through its interpretation maintained the Constitution as a living, growing document through which the Conservative philosophy of orderly change may be preserved.

Conservatives will not always agree with the Supreme Court's rulings. But in its long history, the Court has tended to correct its mistakes and to further the cause of American liberty.

Conservatives should always fight to keep the Court strong and free.

The charge is sometimes made that Conservatives want to freeze the Constitution in the form in which it was handed down to their generation. But this charge is unsupported by the facts. Although they oppose changes made in haste, they have many times supported amendments which were demonstrably in the best interests of the American people.

No better example can be found than the present campaign for a Constitutional amendment to reform the Electoral College, which is being pressed by leading Conservatives.

Under our Electoral College system for electing the President and Vice-President, all the electoral votes of a state are cast for the candidate receiving the greatest number of popular votes. Thus a candidate might carry New York by only a handful of votes and still receive all 45 of that state's electoral votes—enough to cancel out the votes of 10 or more small states.

According to the Congressional Quarterly Service 1961-62 Current American Government manual, "The only principal witnesses (before the Senate Judiciary Constitutional Amendments Subcommittee) opposing a basic overhaul of the current system were representatives of the Kennedy Administration, the Chairman of the Democratic National Committee, and two Senators."

Those supporting basic electoral college reform, said the publication, included former Presidents Hoover, Truman and Eisenhower, 17 Senators, including the Democratic floor leader, one state Governor, professors of law and political science from a large number of universities and several private citizens.

One of the most widely-discussed plans for electoral college reform is the District Plan sponsored by Senator Karl Mundt of South Dakota and co-sponsored by Senators Strom Thurmond of South Carolina, John McClellan of Arkansas, Roman Hruska of Nebraska and Thruston Morton of Kentucky.

This plan would preserve the Electoral College, but would provide for the selection of electors by single-elector districts, with two electors chosen at large in each state. The districts, to be established by the state legislatures, must be composed of contiguous and compact territory and be as nearly equal in population as practicable. If no candidate were to receive a majority of the whole number of electoral votes, the Senate and House, assembled together, would elect from the three candidates receiving the greatest electoral vote.

"The heart of the proposal is that it would end the present disparity now existing in voting weight between citizens of large states and those in small states," says Senator Mundt. "It would modernize the electoral machinery so as to assure that the electoral vote for the Presidency accurately reflects the margin and plurality of the popular vote."

This is but one of several instances in which Conservatives have supported Constitutional change in recent years. Like most Liberals, they recognize the need to change the Constitution whenever changing circumstances indicate a clear need for alteration.

What Conservatives insist upon, however, is that both the letter and spirit of the Constitution—as it exists at any given time—be followed without deviation until such change can be lawfully made.

Why this Conservative reverence for the Constitution?

First, because Conservatives know that only through government by law, and not by men, can our freedoms be guaranteed.

Second, because the Constitution provides for the separation of governmental authority, thus preventing the massive concentration of power always found in totalitarian nations.

And third, because the Constitution is inherently flexible enough to be changed when circumstances and the popular will clearly demand it.

Conservatives oppose the tendencies of both major parties in recent years to let the federal government do "whatever needs to be done," regardless of Constitutional provisions to the contrary. They know that "what needs to be done" at a given moment can only be the judgment of the men in power at the time, and that such judgment should never be allowed to prevail over the accumulated wisdom of the nation's long history.

"The great service of constitutionalism," wrote Clinton Rossiter in his *Conservatism in America*, ". . . is that it forces men to think, talk and compromise before they act. Every constitution is both a grant of power and a catalog of limitations; and the best constitutions lay stress on the latter."

XVII.

■ COMMUNISM PLAYS FOR KEEPS

The aerial reconnaissance photos were unmistakable. America's top military experts studied and evaluated them, and their evaluations were unanimous—Russian missile bases were being constructed throughout Cuba with the utmost haste and secrecy. A lethal weapon, capable of destroying major cities in a third of the nation, was being loaded and cocked just 90 miles from Florida.

During that hectic weekend of October 20-21, 1962, President Kennedy wrestled with the most momentous decision of his administration. Should he consult America's allies? Present the evidence to Khrushchev? Protest to the United Nations? Or should he act boldly, call for a U.S. naval blockade of Cuba, and demand immediate removal of the missiles and bases—or else?

The President had only hours to decide. He summoned military and Congressional leaders to Washington for secret conferences, and then made his dramatic television announcement to the nation at 7 p.m., E.S.T., on October 22: America was standing firm in this crisis, and would risk nuclear war if necessary to put down this newest Russian threat to the Free World.

The American people, virtually with a single voice, cheered his action. Our Latin-American neighbors supported the American "quarantine" of Cuba without a dissenting vote. Our European allies concurred.

And Khrushchev backed down.

The positive action which Conservative spokesmen had for months been demanding in the Cuban situation had been taken, with exactly the results predicted. A more convincing demonstration of the soundness of a firm policy toward Communist aggression could hardly be imagined. Whenever America has stood up to the Communists, the result has been the same. And whenever America has listened to the accommodators and appeasers, Communism has taken another step toward its avowed goal of world domination.

Conservatives rejoice in the obvious changes which hard realities have wrought on the President's foreign policy approach. Once hopeful that he could achieve American goals by dealing and compromising with the Russians, the President has all but abandoned any such strategy.

Time, in its February 2, 1962, issue, reported one milestone in President Kennedy's exodus from accommodation. The President had called together a group of 50 top government leaders, *Time* said, and called to their attention a speech delivered by Khrushchev before a Communist Party rally in Moscow several months earlier.

So significant did the President consider the Khrushchev statement, said *Time,* that he had memorized whole passages of it. He urged every official present to get a copy of the speech and study it.

Among excerpts from the Khrushchev declaration: "There will be liberation wars (Communist terminology for Red-fanned brush fires) as long as imperialism exists, as long as colonialism exists. . . . Such wars are not only justified, they are inevitable, for the colonists do not freely bestow independence on the peoples. . . . Why was it that the U.S. imperialists, who were eager to help the French colonialists, did not venture directly to intervene in the war in Viet Nam? They did not do so because they knew that if they gave the French armed assistance, Viet Nam would receive the same kind of assistance from China, the Soviet Union and other socialist countries, and the fighting could develop into a world war. The outcome of the war is known—North Viet Nam won.

"A similar war is being waged in Algeria today. Or take Cuba. A war was fought there, too. It began as an uprising against a tyrannical regime, backed by U.S. imperialism. Led by Fidel Castro, the people of Cuba won.

"Is there a likelihood of such wars recurring? Yes, there is. . . . What is the attitude of the Marxists to such uprisings? A most favorable attitude. The Communists support just wars of this kind wholeheartedly and without reservations. . . ."

Time summed up its reaction to the impact of the Khrushchev speech on the grim young President in these words:

"If some had already grasped Khrush's message, perhaps sooner than the President himself (who in early 1961 entertained some hopes of an accommodation with the U.S.S.R.), there was nobody tactless enough to bring that up."

Conservatives were heartened by the President's unqualified recognition of the Communist threat. A few weeks later they cheered his decision to resume United States nuclear testing, and his decision to land Marines in Thailand.

If only more Liberals would see the truth about the Communist menace as clearly as has President Kennedy, declare Conservatives, then perhaps America could begin to combat it more effectively.

"We are not fighting Lord Fauntleroy," thundered Senator Strom Thurmond in a Spartanburg, S. C., address on March 17, 1962. "We are fighting the godless, evil, creeping, clawing menace of bolshevism. . . .

"Communism will not change. Communists are not going to become democrats any more than the immutable turning of the earth will cease. Every President from Roosevelt on has tried to improve relations with the Soviet Union. All have tried reason. What did they gain? Khrushchev is just as tough and deceitful today as he has ever been. The subversion is just as intense, their military aggression just as far ranging."

That is the Conservative message on Communism and the threat it poses to America in the 1960s.

We cannot "accommodate" it. We cannot be kind to it. We cannot ignore it and hope that it will go away.

"Victory over Communism is the dominant, proximate goal of American policy," said Senator Goldwater in his much-quoted Air War College address of November 14, 1960. "Proximate in the sense that there are more distant, more 'positive' ends we seek, to which victory over Communism is but a means. But dominant in the sense that every other objective, no matter how worthy intrinsically, must defer to it.

"Peace is a worthy objective; but if we must choose between peace and keeping the Communists out of Berlin, then we must fight. Freedom, in the sense of self-determination, is a worthy objective; but if granting self-determination to the Algerian rebels entails sweeping that area into the Sino-Soviet orbit, then Algerian freedom must be postponed. Justice is a worthy objective; but if justice for Bantus entails driving the government of the Union of South Africa away from the West, then the Bantus must be prepared to carry their identification cards yet a while longer. Prosperity is a worthy objective; but if providing higher standards of living gets in the way of producing sufficient guns to resist Communist aggression, then material sacrifices and denials will have to be made. . . .

"Wherever conflicts arise, they must always be resolved in favor of achieving the indispensable condition for a tolerable world—the absence of Soviet-Communist power."

The Conservative view of the inherent evil of Communism and the necessity of subduing it has remained essentially unchanged since the Russians and Red Chinese set out to conquer the world.

"Communism, from my point of view, denies every principle of Americanism," wrote Senator Taft in his 1951 book, *A Foreign Policy for Americans*. "It denies liberty. Certainly in Soviet Russia there is no one who can be safe from spying and seizure by the Soviet police. Certainly there is none of its boasted equality. . . . Certainly there is no justice. . . . Every man is either for them or against them. Communism denies religion. It denies God Himself. It is hard to find any philosophy which is more the antithesis of American principles, and yet many of our policy makers at Teheran and Yalta seem to have accepted the professions of the Communist leaders as to their interest in liberty, peace, and equality."

And later in the same book: "Whether we have to meet the forces of Communism on the battlefield is open to question. The Russian leaders may be wholly unwilling to trust the entire future of communism to a war, in which Russia, and the Communist leaders, and perhaps communism itself, may be destroyed. . . . And so we have to consider the methods by which we can battle against the spread of communism, and so weaken its spirit that its missionary ardor is destroyed. I believe that can only be done by a positive campaign in behalf of liberty."

The Conservative stand on Communism is not a complicated one:

Communism is opposed to almost every traditional American principle.

Communism is a growing threat to America and the rest of the free world.

We must *win* the battle against Communism.

Why are Conservatives so certain that Communism is a real and terrible threat to freedom in America and throughout the world?

Many Liberal spokesmen do not agree that the Communist threat is either so very real or so very terrible. They cite the declining membership of the American Communist Party, the squabbles between Russia and her satellites, the ideological split between Russia and Red China, the inability of Communist nations to match our production. Arthur Schlesinger, Jr. painted a picture of Communism's philosophical bankruptcy in a May 19, 1962, *Saturday Evening Post* article entitled "The Failure of World Communism."

But Conservatives point to the record of Communist successes since the end of World War II. First China fell, and Chiang Kai-shek was forced to take refuge on the island of Formosa. Then, in a never-ending succession of riots, uprisings and revolts—planned or abetted by Communists—small nations and large were plucked from the pro-Western camp and added to the Red sphere.

"Six years ago (in 1954) French Indo-China, though in trouble, was in the Western camp," said Senator Goldwater in his Air War College address. "Today North Viet Nam is overtly Communist; Laos is teetering between Communism and pro-Communist neutralism; Cambodia is, for all practical purposes, neutralist.

"Indonesia, in the early days of the republic, leaned toward the West. Today Sukarno's government is heavily besieged by avowed Communists, and for all its 'neutralist' pretensions, is a firm ally of Soviet policy.

"Ceylon has moved from a pro-Western orientation to a neutralism openly hostile to the West.

"In the Middle East, Iraq, Syria, and Egypt were, a short while ago, in the Western camp. Today the Nasser and Kassem governments are adamantly hostile to the West, are dependent for their military power on Soviet equipment, and personnel in almost every particular follow the Kremlin's foreign policy line.

"A short time ago all Africa was a Western preserve. . . . Today, Africa is swerving violently away from the West and plunging, it would seem, into the Soviet orbit.

"Latin America was once an area as 'safe' for the West as Nebraska was for Nixon. Today it is up for grabs. One Latin American country, Cuba, has become a Soviet bridgehead 90 miles off our coast. . . .

"Only in Europe have our lines remained firm—and there only on the surface. The strains of neutralism are running strong, notably in England, and even in Germany."

It is hard for Conservatives to see how anyone could fail to recognize this record of Communist expansion as a threat to the United States and to the Free World. Moreover, Communism has been able to instill a missionary zeal in its representatives all over the world. Although their numbers are small—just as they were in 1917 when they grabbed control over all of Russia—Communist agents are able to cripple national economies and infiltrate national governments through sheer force of dedication.

There can be no doubt that Communism is a powerful and a terrible threat to our nation and everything she holds dear.

"What can one do to kindle in the Liberal bosom a spirit of antagonism toward the Communists equal in intensity to that which moved the Liberals to fight against Senator McCarthy?" asked William Buckley, Jr. in his book *Up from Liberalism*. "The horror of the philosophical postulates of Communism has not sufficed, nor the horror of Communism's historical record. What then?

" 'If only,' a witty observer remarked a few years ago, 'Mao Tse-Tung, back in 1946 or 1947, had criticized Margaret Truman's singing! China might have been saved!' "

Buckley's concern over Liberalism's apparent reluctance to mount an all out offensive against Communism is shared by most Conservatives. But those same Conservatives want to be sure the offensive weapons are aimed more accurately than McCarthy aimed them. They know that indiscriminate name-calling and character assassination can endanger the very liberties we are seeking to preserve, set American against American, and weaken our ability to resist the real Communist threat.

Both McCarthy and the extremists in today's anti-Communist movement have rendered a service in promoting a wider knowledge of the Communist threat. But their excesses—particularly in branding as disloyal all who do not share their views—have so disgusted a large number of moderate Americans that the laudable cause of anti-Communism may actually have been weakened because of them.

The thoughtful practitioner of Conservative principles sees many dangers on the radical right. But he sees even more danger on the radical left, with its advocacy of unilateral disarmament, appeasement of Russia, and peace at any cost.

The philosophy of the radical left was admirably summarized in a 1962 publication called *The Liberal Papers.* The book was the result of the so-called "Liberal Project," organized by 12 Liberal Congressmen and announced by Representative Robert Kastenmeier of Wisconsin. In Kastenmeier's words, the project was "a group of Congressmen joined together with a distinguished group of scientists, scholars and experts to formulate new domestic and international policies applicable to the 1960s."

Among the positions stated in *The Liberal Papers,* as summarized by Raymond Moley in the *New York Herald Tribune*: "West Berlin is of no value. . . . Both Germanys should be neutralized militarily . . . NATO should be disestablished . . . the U.S. should abandon nuclear tests . . . trade with Russia should be liberalized . . . the idea that we can avoid war with the Communist world by preparing for it is 'irrational'.

.. We should let the Soviets 'plug in' on our radar warning system.... There should be U.S. recognition and United Nations admission for both Germanys, both Koreas, Communist China and both Vietnams."

House Minority Leader Charles Halleck roared out a protest that the book proposed that "the United States back out of Asia and Europe with our hands up." Senate Minority Leader Everett Dirksen called it "an astounding product." Republican National Chairman William Miller declared the proposals "not only repeat the Communist line—they go beyond the Communist line."

"It's interesting," editorialized Phoenix's Conservative *Arizona Republic,* "in view of the furor raised over right-wing extremists, who occupy no positions of influence within the Federal Government, that all 12 of these appeasers (the sponsors of the Liberal Project) are still in Government. . . .

"The chairman of the project, Marcus Raskin, is presently on the special staff of the National Security Council. . . . We doubt seriously that the nation's newspapers will conduct an all out attack against these left-wing extremists, or that the national magazines and TV networks will devote their resources to unmasking the lunatic left. But they should. For it is here in Congress and in the higher echelons of our Government—not in hometown anti-communist meetings or at anti-communist seminars—where the real danger to our American Republic lies."

Little wonder that the vast majority of American Conservatives, who shun the extremes of both right and left, view the radical left as the most dangerous of the two.

How do Conservatives propose to maintain maximum American effectiveness in the continuing battle against Communism?

First, to encourage every American to understand and appreciate the greatness of his own heritage. It is not enough to be *against* Communism. We must be *for* the American system of government and the American economic system, and we must know why we are for them.

Second, to promote a better understanding of Communism

—its goals, its tactics, and the nature of the threat it poses to America. We must realize that Communism's ultimate goal of world domination has never changed, and that the baffling twists and turns of Communist tactics are not changes in purpose, but calculated moves in the direction of that goal.

Third, to keep America strong—militarily, economically, and morally. If our military shield develops cracks, we invite Communist aggression. If our economy becomes overburdened with excessive taxation, debt and controls, we can lose the battle on the economic front. And if we lose our respect for moral values, our longing for freedom, or our will to oppose Communist tyranny, our enemy may win by default.

Conservative expressions of these basic principles may take many forms. They may be found in the insistence that love of country be expressed in patriotic observances in the schools and in public meetings. They may be expressed in support of Congressional investigation of Communist infiltration. They may crop up in the favoring of loyalty oaths. They may find expression in the insistence that military commanders be permitted to instruct their troops in the nature and danger of Communism, and to speak their minds in public addresses.

Conservatives believe that the more any American learns about his own country and its historic principles—and the more he learns about Communism and the foundations upon which it is built—the more he will appreciate being an American.

It is only with such an appreciation that we can strengthen our resolve to settle for nothing short of victory over Communism in the critical years of decision which lie ahead.

XVIII.
■ ONE GOAL: VICTORY

Seldom before in the world's long history has a nation faced a dilemma so perplexing as that which confronts America today.

On the one hand is the threat of Communist domination, with its sure promise of destruction of the spiritual values and the material blessings which generations of Americans have passed down to us.

On the other hand is the threat of a nuclear war which could in a few days wipe out a billion human beings.

What is the course which can best be relied upon to steer us safely between both unthinkable horrors to a future in which peace and human dignity may reign together?

No question of the 1960s is more vital to America and the Free World, and no question has evoked so much controversy or so many conflicting answers.

Should we accommodate world Communism ... play for time, hoping that somehow the Communists will change ... give ground a little here and a little there to avoid conflict ... and perhaps, when finally forced to the wall, surrender rather than risk destruction?

Or should we proceed boldly ... confront force with superior force ... take the initiative in the ideological, economic and military contest ... risk nuclear war if necessary ... and resolve that nothing short of victory over Communism shall be our goal?

Both courses are risky. But Conservatives are sure that only the latter offers any real promise of a tolerable future for ourselves and our children.

"This Republic, and the freedom for which it stands, was born in the decision that *how* a nation survives is as important as *whether* it survives," declared a 1960 Special Task Force Report prepared for the House Republican Committee by a group of leading experts on world affairs. "If a nation doubts its mission in the world, it will regress and cease to retain the confidence of anyone. . . . History abounds with examples of nations forced both to fight and surrender because of failure to convince an enemy that it will not only live for its ideals, but is prepared to *die* for them."

The Conservative Democrat view on what course America must take in foreign relations was expressed in a March, 1962, address by Senator Strom Thurmond. "We want peace, but peace with freedom and justice," he said. "The Communists want the world. If they get it, there won't be any peace for anybody, including those who say they would rather be Red than dead. If we want peace at any price, this is cheap, and can be attained without a struggle."

On this point, Conservatives are unanimously agreed: Mere survival is not a worthy goal of free men, and peace is priced too high when purchased at the cost of liberty and human dignity.

What do Conservatives mean when they insist that U.S. foreign policy should be one aimed at victory over Communism—a "win" policy, as opposed to the "no-win" policy which too often is advocated by Liberals?

If the Liberal policy is a "no-win" policy, does it necessarily follow that Liberals advocate abject surrender to Communism?

There are those among the right-wing extremists who insist that surrender is indeed the Liberal aim, and that Liberal leaders are, therefore, guilty of high treason.

But this is not the generally-held Conservative view.

Senator Goldwater, in his *Conscience of a Conservative*, made a clear differentiation between the views of the radical right and those of most Conservatives regarding this "no-win" policy.

"It is clear that our national leadership over the past four years has favored neither surrender nor treason. It is equally clear, however, that our leaders have not made *victory* the goal of American policy. And the reason that they have ot done so, I am saying, is that they have never believed that the Communists are in earnest.

"Our avowed national objective is 'peace.' We have, with great sincerity, 'waged' peace, while the Communists wage war. We have sought 'settlements' while the Communists seek victories. We have tried to pacify the world. The Communists mean to own it. Here is why the contest has become an unequal one, and why, essentially, we are losing it."

When Conservatives insist on a "win" foreign policy, they are not—as some Liberals have declared—insisting that America must engage the Communist world in armed conflict.

What Conservatives *do* mean is that we have been, and are now, in a life-or-death Cold War with Communism on many fronts, and we must win that Cold War. Our policy must not be one of maintaining the status quo, or of simply "containing" Communism. It must be one of *victory* on every front—political, diplomatic, ideological, economic, psychological and military.

Our goal of victory will have been achieved when Communism no longer has the capability of threatening the peace and freedom of the world. The Conservative concept of victory does not include subjugation of Communist nations to our will, or the forcing of our republican form of government and our capitalistic economic system on any nation which does not want them. But that concept of victory *does* envision a world in which differing political and economic systems are free to flourish and compete in peace, and in which nations may enjoy self-determination without the fear of Communist aggression from within or without.

Such a free and peaceful competition of ideologies will not be possible so long as Communism maintains its determination to dominate the world and possesses the power to press forward toward that domination. Conservatives believe that only by maintaining superior military forces as a shield against attack, and by demonstrating to the world the superiority of free government and a free economy, can we hasten the disintegration of Communism throughout the world.

The Communists have long understood the nature of the world conflict in which we are engaged. Every move they have made for decades has been aimed at one goal—victory. And that basic understanding has led to triumph after triumph in the years since World War II.

The Communists are not supermen. They have weaknesses and problems and dissensions, just as we do. Moreover, they lack our tradition of industrial know-how and productivity, built up in a century and a half of technological development. But they have a single-minded devotion to the goal of victory over all opposition, and that has proved to be a mighty weapon.

Not until America and the West can match the Communist will to *win* can we regain the initiative.

How do Conservatives propose that America can best move forward toward a complete—and peaceful—victory in the Cold War? We can do so: BY BOLSTERING OUR POSITION AS THE STRONGEST NATION ON EARTH.

Aggressors throughout recorded history have attacked only when their victims have allowed themselves to become militarily weak, and when that weakness has offered a reasonable hope that aggression would be successful.

We do not increase the risk of war by building up our atomic arsenal, by keeping our military forces trained and ready. We could invite war in no better way than to disarm to the extent that our Communist enemy would become convinced that aggression could succeed.

Robert G. Neumann, director of the Institute of International and Foreign Studies of the University of California at Los Angeles, has described the danger in this way:

"Whether we like it or not, we cannot afford to lose sight of the fact . . . that despite all tension and provocation, full-fledged war is not likely to break out, is primarily due to (the) 'balance of terror' which has made it very unsafe for an aggressor to unleash atomic war. If, by the same token, disarmament were to be undertaken in such a way as to gravely upset this balance, either by being too unilateral or by being too uncontrolled, then such action would . . . immeasurably increase the fearful danger of war."

American military strength must be bolstered in every possible way—by testing our atomic weapons when necessary, by developing new weapons, by improving our readiness for limited wars, by maintaining our regular and reserve forces at the highest level our economy can support, by providing military assistance to our allies.

But military preparedness is not our only source of national strength. We must keep our productive capacity growing by maintaining an economic climate in which there is increasing incentive to build new plants, develop new productive techniques, and replace obsolete machinery.

We must keep taxation and the national debt under control, in order that inflation and financial collapse may not rob us of all our hard-won gains on the economic and military fronts.

And, perhaps most important, we must bolster our moral armaments—the appreciation of our national heritage, our determination to fight for justice and freedom, and our will to win no matter what sacrifices may be demanded.

A strong and determined America has little to fear from any aggressor.

BY TAKING THE OFFENSIVE IN THE COLD WAR.

"We must commence to take actions designed to put the Kremlin off balance," declared Rep. Glenard P. Lipscomb of California in an address before the House of Representatives on September 27, 1961. "We must take every advantage offered us by the seething unrest in the satellites and in Red China. We must expose to the world the vast weaknesses of the Sino-Soviet bloc rather than to help to propagandize their unproven strengths and shabby circus tricks."

Rep. Lipscomb is only one of many Conservative spokesmen who urge that we quit our defensive tactics and move boldly to the offense in the Cold War.

"The central strategic fact of the Cold War, as it is presently fought, is that the Communists are on the offensive and we are on the defensive," Senator Goldwater has said. "The Soviet Union is always moving ahead, trying to get something from the free world; the West endeavors, at best, to hold what it has. . . . Given the dynamic, revolutionary character of the enemy's challenge, we cannot win merely by trying to hold our own. In addition to parrying his blows we must strike our own.... We must always try to engage the enemy at times and places, and with weapons, of our own choosing."

Conservatives are weary of defensive strategy. They believe our only hope lies in taking the initiative, despite the apparent risks involved.

How, specifically, do Conservatives propose that we take the offensive in the Cold War?

More than a decade ago, Senator Taft suggested these steps:

"1. We can conduct a world-wide propaganda in behalf of liberty.... In the Voice of America we have already adopted the general principle.... We should find those people among the citizens of each (Communist-dominated) nation who agree with our principles and finance them to put on an effective propaganda.

"2.... Somewhere in our Government there ought to be an agency completely advised as to the character and identity of all those forces and individuals fighting for freedom throughout the Communist world. Such an agency should be able to organize these forces to play a vital role, in war and in peace, in the ultimate undermining of the Communist conspiracy.

"3. Everywhere throughout the world we should encourage and build up those forces in friendly countries or neutral countries which believe in liberty and are prepared to battle against Communism."

Today, direct action in the world's trouble spots is advocated by many Conservatives.

"What can we do?" asks Senator Thurmond.

"We can blockade Cuba, particularly if the current actions don't bring Castro to his knees very soon....

"We can tell West Berlin that we are with them all the way in freeing East Berlin....

"We can quit trading with Communist nations; quit sending them aid....

"Naïvete, and later a faint heart, lost us Cuba. One tank against a row of cinder blocks might have saved us from a Berlin wall. Our own recent history has proved that we do not have war every time Russia rattles a rocket. In Lebanon, we moved with courage and force, and we did not go to war. In Formosa, we sailed the Seventh Fleet into the troubled

eas and told the communists to try to climb over it. In Berlin
ve airlifted the free world's hopes and we did not go to war."

We cannot win the Cold War by defensive strategy, say the
Conservatives. We can win only by going on the offensive
nd staying there.

Y LIMITING FOREIGN AID ONLY TO OUR ALLIES.

The Conservative position on foreign aid is that such aid
hould be given only where it bolsters our allies in the global
attle against Communism.

"The United States should support its friends abroad and
istinguish between its allies and those practicing a question-
ble form of neutralism," declared Senator Mundt in a De-
ember 21, 1961, address. "We should reduce American
xpenditures abroad; eliminate waste; and provide more
uidance and technical assistance rather than so much dollar
id."

Since the end of World War II, the United States has
pent about $90 billion on foreign aid, and today is spending
5 billion per year for that purpose. According to *Time* of
March 23, 1962, "nearly every non-Communist nation in the
vorld gets some U.S. aid—economic, military or both—the
nly important exceptions being Canada, the Republic of
outh Africa and the traditional European neutrals, Swit-
erland, Sweden and Ireland. . . . Economic aid goes mainly
o the 'under-developed,' mostly neutralist nations of Africa,
Asia and Latin America. Military aid goes mainly to NATO
nembers and to pro-Western or Communist-menaced nations
f the Far East."

What alarms many Conservatives is not just the universal
nd indiscriminate nature of U.S. foreign aid, but the fact
hat Communist nations and openly hostile "neutrals" have
een among the recipients. Communist Yugoslavia, whose
ilots we are training in the United States, will receive aid
n fiscal 1963. India, which gobbled up Portuguese Goa;
ndonesia, which threatens to invade Dutch New Guinea; and
Jasser's Egypt, hardly a friend of the West—all these will
et help from U. S. taxpayers in 1963.

Conservatives have supported some forms of foreign aid—
articularly military and technical assistance to nations

pledged to oppose Communist advances—but they are hopeful that aid programs need not continue indefinitely.

"I have always said that I look forward to the day in which foreign aid of all kinds will become unnecessary," Arizona's Rep. John Rhodes wrote in his newsletter of September 14, 1961. "I have always done my level best to keep it to a minimum and to keep it out of Communist hands."

Even former Secretary of Commerce Charles Sawyer, who helped set up the Marshall Plan for European aid, became disillusioned when he saw that foreign aid was fast becoming a permanent fixture in U.S. foreign policy.

"Permanent strength and stability for the Western European allies do not lie in continuing U.S. subsidies and grants, but in expanding production and trade," said Sawyer in a 1952 statement. "Indefinite dependence on aid destroys self-respect, impairs the real strength of the recipient economy and has a capacity to destroy friendly relations between the giver and the recipient."

Like any giveaway program, foreign aid is almost impossible to halt once it has been started. The recipients protest. The diplomats of the State Department protest. The more than 40,000 persons employed in handling foreign aid funds protest. And so the pressures mount to extend and expand the multi-billion dollar program.

Conservatives look more favorably on such aid programs as the Peace Corps, which has some 700 volunteers giving technical assistance in nations which request it. As a result, the House, on April 3, 1962, thundered its approval, 317 votes to 70, of a bill enlarging the Peace Corps.

Typical of the reaction of early Peace Corps opponents was the statement of Rep. Howard D. Smith of Virginia, who was quoted in *Congressional Quarterly* as saying: "I have taken care to read what I could about the performance of this program as it went along and I am happy to say I think they have done a good job."

Smith was among those who changed his vote in 1962 and supported the Peace Corps.

Conservatives do not oppose all assistance to foreign nations. But they want to gradually reduce its cost, substitute technical assistance for dollar gifts where possible, and plan for the day when it may be ended. Most important, they want to be sure that such aid is used to combat Communism, not to give it assistance.

BY RE-EXAMINING OUR ATTITUDE TOWARD THE UNITED NATIONS.

Conservatives, long concerned over Liberal pressures to subordinate United States sovereignty to the collective will of the United Nations, were elated when Washington's Liberal Senator Henry Jackson hoisted a warning signal on March 20, 1962.

"The United States should take a more restricted view of the United Nations' capacity for helpfulness," Senator Jackson told the National Press Club. "The United Nations is an important avenue of American foreign policy. Yet practices have developed which, I believe, lead to an undue influence of U.N. considerations in our national decision making. . . . We must remember that the U.N. is not a substitute for national policies wisely conceived to uphold our vital interest."

Conservatives had been saying virtually the same thing, in stronger language, for some time.

Senator Byrd made a special trip to San Francisco during the conference establishing the United Nations in 1945 for the sole purpose of arguing against the veto provision. From the moment the veto concept was adopted as part of the United Nations machinery, Senator Byrd and many other Conservatives were certain that the UN could not, in itself, be a wholly effective agency for keeping the peace.

Among those who shared the Virginia senator's view was Senator Taft, who stated in a 1952 *Collier's* interview that: "My own view is that an international organization can only be effective if there is no veto power."

Like many other Conservatives, Senator Taft saw important values in the UN. "The United Nations has a real use in trying to prevent war by persuasion, by consultation and by bringing causes of war out into the open where they can be seen and perhaps resolved," he said in the *Collier's* interview. But on many occasions he pointed out the danger of entrusting to the UN the making of United States foreign policy.

The other great powers—and the Soviet Union in particular—have long recognized the need to act in their own best interests, even when those interests conflict with UN policy. Conservatives believe that the United States should maintain that same right.

"The United Nations has its useful functions, but the formulation and conduct of American policy is not among them," Senator Goldwater said in his Air War College address of 1960. "On past occasions, when we have subordinated to United Nations policy our own notions of how to wage the cold war effectively, Western interests have suffered—the Korean War, the Suez crisis, the Iraqui revolution, this year's events in the Congo, and many others . . . There may be occasions when the United Nations can be utilized to provide a broad base of policies that further Western interests. But when submission of a matter to the United Nations will predictably muddy the waters and obstruct the pursuit of American policy, then we must, as we did in the case of Berlin, quietly insist on settling the problem elsewhere."

There are those Conservative spokesmen who advocate immediate United States withdrawal from the United Nations. Even the *Saturday Evening Post,* hardly a radical right-wing publication, editorialized on October 28, 1961, that failure of the UN "could be the foundation of firmer unity among nations threatened by Communism. This unity has been lacking, but, if it could be achieved, it would dispel the Communist dream of world conquest once and for all."

Conservatives, generally speaking, do not wish to see the United Nations fail, nor do they advocate United States withdrawal.

But Conservatives doubt that the United States should continue to provide the major part of UN financing. As of November 30, 1961, according to *Saturday Review,* only the United States and 12 small nations had paid their UN assessments in full. Russia, the nation farthest in arrears, owed most of its annual budget assessment, plus $12,774,084 for the UN Emergency Force and $20,088,253 for its Congo action assessment.

It was partly for that reason that most Conservatives opposed the President's request that the United States purchase half of a proposed $200,000,000 United Nations' bond issue—

particularly since $32,000,000 of the UN debt was owed to the United States.

"It occurs to me that if the United Nations is going to succeed," said Senator Tower on March 18, 1962, ". . . then all nations must be concerned with the United Nations, and they must be prepared to support the United Nations. And it appears that so many nations have taken their obligations to the UN pretty lightly."

The United Nations, founded with such high hopes in 1945, has had some notable successes to counterbalance its many failures. It may serve as a force for the maintenance of world peace in the future. But, Conservatives are sure, it is not likely to succeed until the major nations of the world regard it highly enough to pay their fair share for its support.

The time has come to re-examine our role in the United Nations—to determine whether we have not leaned too heavily upon it and have not already subordinated too much of our national sovereignty to the UN will. Conservatives hope that more Liberal leaders will join Senator Jackson in asking that we not permit "undue influence of U.N. considerations in our national decision making."

Conservative proposals for winning the Cold War are many, but they follow a single pattern which stresses national strength and a determination to take and hold the offensive.

Among the Conservative positions on today's Cold War problems:

Efforts to court favorable world opinion—Nations, like people, want their neighbors to think well of them; but it can be disastrous for a nation to fashion its foreign policy with world opinion as a principal consideration. The United States has great power, and it must use that power firmly and effectively against the Communist menace. No course we may pursue will please all our world neighbors, and we should not be unduly concerned about whether the course we choose pleases or displeases them.

Use of regional alliances—Such alliances as the North Atlantic Treaty Organization (NATO) and the Southeast Asia Treaty Organization (SEATO) have served as powerful deterrents to Communist aggression. They must be strengthened. Moreover, they should serve not only as a shield against Communism, but as a collective force dedicated to pushing back our common Cold War enemy.

The value of negotiation with the Communists—Recent history has proved that the Communists are willing to negotiate only about rights and territory which are already ours. They regard negotiation solely as a tool for furthering their own interests, and break agreements whenever it will serve those interests. Normal diplomatic channels of communication should be kept open, but we should be wary of being pressured into "summit" meetings and other special conferences which the Communists have in the past used primarily for propaganda purposes.

Recognition and UN admission for Red China—In Korea, in Tibet, in Laos and on many other fronts, Red China has made war on free peoples or on the UN itself. Recognition or UN admission would place a stamp of respectability on a nation which has behaved like an international outlaw. It would discourage resistance on the part of our friends in Asia, and would make it virtually impossible for the UN to make any effective progress toward world peace.

The Freedom Academy Proposal—The nation has no adequate means for training personnel to wage political warfare of the kind needed in the Cold War. Senator Mundt has sponsored a bill creating a Freedom Academy for this purpose. The bill passed the Senate in 1961, but it has not been acted upon by the House. As Roscoe Drummond pointed out in his May 27, 1962, column, "The Senate Judiciary Committee . . . considers this bill to be one of the most important ever introduced in the Congress. . . . It has broad bipartisan backing, including Republican Senators Case, Goldwater, Fong, Butler, Hickenlooper, Miller and Keating and Democratic Senators Douglas, Dodd, Smathers and Proxmire." Conservatives support the Freedom Academy bill, and they have been joined in that support by many Liberals.

To summarize Conservative positions on foreign policy: America faces grave risks in either a "soft" or a "hard" approach to the problem of combatting the spread of world Communism. But the latter offers the better hope of success, and in the long run is less likely to lead to nuclear war. We must aim for maximum American strength—military, economic and moral. We must help our allies in our common battle against Communism, but should be more discriminate in our foreign aid. We must recognize the limitations of the United Nations as an agency for combatting world Communism and not surrender to the UN our responsibility for the conduct of American foreign policy. We must not be unduly sensitive to world opinion, not to Communist pressures for useless negotiation.

Most important of all, we must realize—as the Communists have long realized—that we are in a life-or-death battle which will affect the future course of world history.

And we must win.

4.

Conservative Goals for America

XIX.

■ THE FRUITS OF FREEDOM

In his unforgettable novel, *Brave New World*, Aldous Huxley painted a vivid picture of the world of tomorrow—based on the assumption that Twentieth Century trends away from individual freedom and toward centralized planning and control would continue to their logical ends.

In Huxley's world of the future, human beings were to be conceived in Government hatcheries, their mental and physical capacities exactly controlled by formula. There were to be variations in ability, of course, because some men had to be bred to conduct scientific research and others to sweep out Government factories and collect garbage. But the central Government was to decide how many were to be bred as "Alphas" (superior intellects), how many as "Epsilons" (dull but willing laborers), and how many in the classes in between.

It was to be in some ways a wonderful world—a world without hunger or poverty, a world without war, a world without frustrations or unfulfilled desires. No man would have to compete with any other, because the central Government satisfied all his wants. Life would proceed calmly and uneventfully from one century to the next. And, in the eventuality that someone should become bored or unhappy in any way, he would be issued a supply of a tranquilizer called "soma," which would immediately restore him to a state of relaxed happiness.

But the horrors of such a world glower on every page of Huxley's book.

No challenges face a man at the beginning of each new day, because the Government has made it impossible for him either to succeed magnificently or fail crushingly. There is no God except technology and no loyalty except to the all-powerful State. There are State-provided amusements by the score, but no real happiness. All deviations from normal be havior are eliminated by scientific conditioning, and any stir ring of desire to rise above one's niche in life is immediatel detected and smothered.

Life stretches ahead in a dreary, featureless plain. And al because the only really indispensable ingredient of life—free dom—has been eliminated.

When he wrote the book in 1932, Huxley projected it 60 years into the future. But he has since revised his estimate. "Today," he wrote in a preface to a more recent edition, "i seems quite possible that the horror may be upon us within a single century."

Theorizing about Utopias has never been very popular with Conservative advocates because they think in terms of wha is possible, not what might be ideal.

Conservatives believe that no way of life would be tol erable without freedom of individual choice and action. An so long as men are free to strive and compete—to succee and fail—there will be both triumph and disappointment in an scheme of things.

But, assuming that an ideal society is not likely to be at tained in the foreseeable future, what kind of America ar Conservatives striving to build?

It would be a far cry from the super-State envisioned i *Brave New World*.

Its citizens—instead of being preconditioned, propagandize puppets of the Establishment—would be self-reliant indi viduals whose differences in personality would be recognize and cherished by society.

Its central government would be dedicated, not to the sup plying of all the people's wants, but to the creation of a economic climate in which each citizen would have maximum opportunity to supply his own needs, together with as man luxuries as his energies and abilities might earn for him.

Its diety would be God, not technology or social stability

And freedom—freedom to aspire, to be different, to achiev greatness, to fail—would be honored far above any se

curity which might be gained by submission to the will of
the State.

Would there be collective action? Of course. But it would
be the collective action of free men joining together willingly
in labor unions and employer groups, in agricultural associations and professional societies, in local and national
charitable foundations. Government at all levels would necessarily be by collective action, but it would be based on law
and would guarantee the rights of individuals and minority
groups.

Can such a free society be possible in the future, despite
the enormous pressures which appear to be forcing America
toward the concept of the super-State?

Conservatives are sure it can be—and must be—if the
world of tomorrow is to be a tolerable place in which to live.

What kind of America do Conservatives envision as the
Twentieth Century gives way to the Twenty-First?

If the courses advocated by Conservative spokesmen in
earlier chapters win general acceptance, the United States of
the year 2000 might be described in this way by a con-
temporary journalist:

Federal Government—It is strong, responsive to the will
of the people, and firmly based on the principles of the Constitution. Its functions are those granted by the Constitution,
as amended by the people and interpreted by their courts,
and those functions are not allowed to encroach on the responsibilities reserved by the Constitution to state and local
governments.

The federal government in domestic matters acts primarily
as an umpire, not as an active participant. It enforces the
rules under which our economy can best grow and prosper,
moving swiftly to remove obstacles to free competitive enterprise whether those obstacles are erected by either management or labor. It safeguards the Constitutional rights of all
citizens whenever they are threatened.

In foreign affairs it provides for the defense of the nation
and represents the American people in their dealings with
the world community. It acts, in cooperation with other free

nations, in combatting any force which may threaten the peace and freedom of the world.

But the federal government does *not* attempt to guarantee its citizens' welfare or prosperity. It does *not* tamper with the laws of supply and demand. As a result, it is smaller, less expensive and less a threat to the freedom of its citizens than it was 40 years ago.

State and Local Governments—Recognizing that it was not enough simply to curb the activities of the federal government, state and local governments long ago assumed the many responsibilities they had been surrendering to Washington. There has been a rebirth in interest in home rule, and a new determination to make it work.

Citizens groups have been working for the rewriting of archaic state constitutions and local charters to make them applicable to the present. The most capable leaders in private life now have thrown off their distaste for politics and willingly serve on city councils and in state legislatures.

Taxpayers support local bond issues and state tax programs, knowing that it will cost less in the long run to act on the local and state level than to turn problems over to the federal government.

Taxing and Spending—Federal taxes are now lower and taxes on local levels a little higher, but the net result is a saving to the individual and corporate taxpayer. Thus more money is available to invest in the tools of production, in consumer goods, in life and health insurance, in charitable projects.

America's citizens are at last educated to the fact that no government service is "free," and they make it clear to every Congressman and legislator that extravagant spending is not to be tolerated. The technique of "tax, spend, and elect" is now only a memory from the past.

Pay-as-you-go financing has returned to favor, and the national debt has been gradually reduced to a manageable level. A major cause of inflation thus has been removed.

Welfare—Once the crushing load of taxation and control was lightened, the American economy moved ahead so rapidly that virtually every working-age citizen who wants one now has a job. He has a standard of living higher than could have been imagined 40 years ago, and savings to tide him over times of misfortune.

Those who remain unable to provide for themselves are helped by private charities and by agencies of the state and local governments. Only when every other possibility has been exhausted does the federal government enter the welfare picture, and then only until lower levels of government can resume the load.

No American is permitted to exist in hardship. But welfare payments are not sufficient to tempt anyone to trade a life of self-reliance for that of a permanent government ward.

Labor—In the now discredited super-State, labor unionism was one of the first victims, since free association of workers to bargain collectively could not be tolerated in a society which is planned from the top. Free and vigorous labor unions, therefore, play a major role in the economy of this year 2000.

Labor is the working partner—not the master—of management. Anti-monopoly legislation applies equally to both partners, and dangerous accumulations of power are not permitted to either.

Education—The "Neo-Pavlovian Conditioning Rooms" envisioned by Huxley's *Brave New World* were to shape the thinking of children from birth, and the state was to furnish and control all education. These concepts are recognized today as highly dangerous to freedom.

We now believe it is essential to keep the planning and financing of education on the local level. Local school districts provide the facilities and shape the curricula for the elementary and high schools, in cooperation with the state governments. Taxpayers, recognizing that they pay the bill whether the federal or local government assumes the responsibility for educational financing, have been giving increased support to their school districts to head off the threat of federal control.

Federal support of higher education is limited to the encouragement of basic and applied research, to loans for construction on college campuses, to the collection and dissemination of new knowledge discovered by scholars, and to other activities which will encourage education without controlling it.

The National Economy—Long experimentation with government controls has shown us that no better economic system could be devised than the free functioning of the marketplace. Without the expenditure of a cent of taxpayers' money, it establishes production levels, prices, and wages. Moreover, it does so rapidly, and in response to consumer desires.

The federal government regulates the economy to protect the public interest, but it does not attempt to plan and control it. Once government stepped out of the business of subsidizing, wage-fixing, quota setting, and all its other attempts to overrule the laws of supply and demand, the "farm problem" and other economic imbalances gradually disappeared.

The federal government has removed itself from competition with private enterprise. With every means at its disposal, it encourages investment in new productive machinery and the creation of additional jobs. It recognizes the necessity of operating business at a profit.

Freed from artificial planning, the American economy now produces and distributes enough goods and services to make every man wealthy by mid-Twentieth Century standards.

Civil Rights—America is fast becoming a nation in which citizens of all races and religions live and work together in brotherhood. The gains made during the Twentieth Century have all but eliminated religious bigotry and have brought new dignity to minority races.

The federal government protects the Constitutional rights of all citizens, and sets an example of nondiscrimination in its own activities. But it does not attempt to force total racial integration in areas of the nation in which the majority is not yet ready to accept it.

The Negro has increased his own chances for complete acceptance through self-improvement and patient effort toward social equality. And mutual understanding has broken down many of the economic barriers which once obstructed that self-improvement.

Progress has been made through evolution, and not through force, coercion or government edict.

The Constitution—Now, more than ever before, America honors the Constitution and the principle of government by law. Former tendencies of the federal government to encroach on the Constitutional powers of the states have been halted by a better popular understanding of the dangers involved. Within the federal government, balance of the Legislative, Executive and Judicial branches has been regained.

The Constitutionality of any proposed program is now the first consideration. And every effort is being made to keep the Constitution abreast of changing times and applicable to the needs of the American people.

Foreign Policy—The downfall of world Communism, which had been started in the mid-1960s when the United States led the Free World in a determined Cold War offensive, was virtually complete by the mid-1970s. In this year 2000, historians can look back with enough perspective to pinpoint the decisive battles. There was the economic victory, spurred on by Capitalism's superior productive powers, the success of the Common Market, and the collapse of Russian and Red Chinese agriculture. There was the ideological victory, gained when free nations were at last able to demonstrate to the uncommitted nations and to the Communist-dominated peoples alike the superiority of free government. And finally, there was the massive military confrontation, which convinced Communist leaders that further aggression would be suicidal.

There remains no serious threat of world war. Men came to realize that atomic weapons could not be banned, any more than crossbows or gun powder could have been banned in earlier ages, and nuclear weapons are being maintained as a powerful deterrent to aggression on the part of any ambitious nation. But military forces are now much smaller and less expensive.

The United Nations, which was maintained as an agency for the exchange of ideas and the furthering of international understanding, is now held in high regard throughout the world. Its international police force, which now supplements the military establishments of the individual nations instead of attempting to serve as a substitute for them, stands ready to snuff out local brush fires before they can spread into world conflagrations.

Self-determination of nations is now guaranteed, and there are many different political and economic systems thriving in peaceful competition. The worldwide spread of modern productive and distributive techniques has all but conquered hunger and want, even though the world population has increased enormously.

The world in 2000 can look forward to a century of peaceful progress, both here and throughout the newly-explored Solar System.

What are the fruits of freedom—of a society in which Conservative principles prevail?

In the realm of material things, the list would be endless, because it is under free enterprise that goods and services for the satisfaction of human wants are produced in the greatest possible abundance. A comparable abundance is not possible in any other system, and particularly not in systems which substitute artificial schemes for wealth distribution in the place of individual desire for gain.

In the area of government, the Conservative principle of decentralized responsibility offers the best hope for keeping government always responsive to the will of the people. It is when too much power becomes concentrated in government agencies too big, too complex, too far away and too insulated from the protests of the voter that government becomes the master, not the servant, of its citizens.

But it is in the preservation of freedom itself that Conservative principles guarantee their greatest rewards. Even if the free economy did not produce a higher standard of living, and even if decentralized authority did not offer the most responsive and efficient form of government, the blessings of freedom which are inherent in Conservative principles still would weight the scales heavily in their favor.

What kind of America does the future hold in store?

A prosperous America, an efficiently governed America, a

peaceful America, an America imbued with the highest spiritual values and sensitive to the needs of all its citizens.

But most of all, Conservatives vow, an America in which all men are free.

XX.

■ THE KEY MAN—YOU

The letter to *Newsweek*'s Raymond Moley was in unmistakably feminine handwriting. The postmark was that of a small town in Illinois, and the date was shortly before the 1960 elections.

"This is the first year I have been able to vote," it said, "and consequently it is the first time I have paid any attention to what is going on in politics. Both my husband and I are anxious to DO something. But we don't know what to do."

Newly-motivated Conservatives all over the nation can understand and share the frustrations of this young woman. Whether our first vote was cast in 1960, or 1892, or is yet to be cast, we share her desire to DO something.

But what? And how? As one individual in 180,000,000, can any of us do anything at all to change America?

The answer is a resounding YES. One politically-oriented citizen can change the course of a local election, and the people he influences in his adult life may be counted in the thousands. Even two or three more such citizens in each of our 125,000 precincts would create a political force which could shake the most firmly-entrenched political regime and shape the governmental philosophy of the nation for decades to come.

Moley pointed all this out in his reply to the lady from Illinois, and advised her and her husband to do these things: 1—Become active in the local organization of the party of their choice: 2—Invite small groups to their home to discuss candidates and issues; 3—Organize similar meetings in other homes; 4—Obtain and distribute literature from party headquarters; 5—Do whatever work the party might require; telephoning, ringing doorbells, mailing letters, speak-

ng, or any of a dozen others; 6—Help raise money; 7—
Get out the vote on election day.

"The average citizen's one vote does count," said Paul
Van Riper in his popular *Handbook of Practical Politics*. "But
when he also becomes a political worker, he can multiply
his effectiveness many fold. Not only does he vote himself,
but he makes himself a committee of one to see that others,
who have that hopeless feeling about their votes, snap out
of it and go to the polls. . . .

"He tells the men and women in the shop or office. . . .
He goes to work on his Sunday School class, the fellows at the
lodge, the other veterans in the post, the members of his
union. *He gets them to vote. . . .*

"Even a 'bad' politician will stop, look and listen if it
takes a big number of votes to elect him over his opponent.
That means that a lot of people will have to be kept pleased
or he'll be out of luck next time—and politicians are always
thinking of next time."

How can Conservative principles, so widely held in America,
be translated into political action?

How can individual Conservatives—without political experience—without money—without much influence in the community—start moving America back onto the road toward
local responsibility and individual freedom?

It is easy to lose heart and quit the battle before it is
begun. Liberalism is too firmly entrenched, we may say. The
awesome magnitude of the Federal Establishment is so overwhelming that it can never be reduced. Maybe it would be
better to spare ourselves the struggle, to sit down and wait
for the inevitable coming of the super-State and the first
government distribution of soma.

But all across the land Conservatives are deciding, not
to surrender, but to fight. They are rousing themselves out of
their lethargy in such numbers that the architects of the welfare state already are crying out in alarm.

The issues are clear. The battle plans have been drawn
up. The leaders are in the field. All that is needed now is

for several million more Conservatively-inclined Americans to leave the sidelines and join the fray.

The key man today is *you*—the citizen who has become convinced that America's best hope for the future lies in Conservative principles and who is willing to do something about it.

"The task cannot be accomplished by those elected officials who support Constitutional principles, for there are far too few of us," Senator Thurmond told the Minneapolis Conservative Citizens Committee in a 1961 address. "And even were we legion in number, our success would still depend on the actions which must replace the apathy of the general public."

What can *you* do?

Let us consider some of the most urgent needs:

1. *To Take a Firm Stand for Your Beliefs*. Before anything worthwhile can be accomplished, there must be desire and a firm resolve. Until you leave the ranks of the uncommitted nonpartisans, a majority of whom have simply never taken the trouble to take stock of *what,* if anything, they do believe about American government and its future, you can do little of value. Once you decide that Conservative principles are worth fighting and sacrificing for, the next steps follow logically.

2. *To Study and Learn*. Instincts and vague preferences are not enough to sustain really effective action. You must know what Conservatism is all about and *why* it offers the best solutions to the problems of the 1960s.

What to study? You could start by exploring the writings of Edmund Burke, Alexander Hamilton, James Madison and Thomas Jefferson. You could re-read the Constitution, perhaps for the first time since school days. You could learn what principles motivated John C. Calhoun and Benjamin Disraeli. The written legacy of Robert Taft in the modern era offers much intellectual nourishment. And certainly you should know what today's Conservative leaders are saying and how they are voting—study current legislative proposals—read both sides of the Great Debate as it unfolds in the newspapers and news magazines.

3. *To Make Your Views Known to Your Elected Officials*. Virtually every elected official sincerely wants to carry out

he will of the people who put him in office. But they cannot now what your will is unless you tell them.

"No king ever wielded a scepter more powerful than a -cent pencil in the hands of an American citizen when he its down to write his Congressman or Senator," said the irst *Hoover Report*. "Letters have a powerful impact," ays Senator Mundt, "whether they are sent to your Congresional representatives, to your newspaper, *or to the President*."

Each letter to a lawmaker carries weight. And if a citizen an talk a dozen friends into writing, too, the impact could e just enough to change a vote on a bill.

Representative Richard H. Poff of Virginia, who often ells his constituents how vital he considers their letters, has isted seven suggestions for giving correspondence maximum ffectiveness: "1—A letter is better than a phone call; 2—Make your letter brief; 3—Confine your comments to one ubject for each letter; 4—Outline the reasons for your posiion; 5—Don't insult your Congressman with promises or hreats; 6—A personal letter is better than a form letter r a signature on a petition; 7—Refuse to accept an unesponsive reply."

Don't forget that local and state officials need your guidnce, too. Your representative in the State Legislature, once e had recovered from the shock of having a constituent call n him, will be happy to hear your views and discuss ssues with you. And anyone who has ever seen the typically poor public attendance at city council and school board neetings knows how easy it can be for one articulate visior to influence action on the local level.

4. *To Become an Active Worker in Your Political Party*. You may not agree with the entire program of either najor political party in your state, but it is a political act of life that little is accomplished by "splinter" parties.

The best hope for Conservatives is to become active in the xisting party organization and try to influence it conservaively.

"A number of people who call themselves conservatives old that the Republican Party can be made more conservaive by (their) remaining outside its ranks," said the Indiana

State Central Republican Committee in a 1962 issue of it publication *Republican Counterattack*. "The Republican Party's complexion is determined by those who join its local units, and prove their value by hard work ... not by thos who remain aloof and seek its defeat."

The same might be said with equal truth about th Democratic Party.

Bulky books have been written about how to become politically effective citizen through party work. The America Heritage Foundation's little pamphlet *Who, Me, a Politician* outlines some of the work which needs to be done, and ex plains it as well as any other publication.

"The first step," it says, "is to talk to someone who i already active. ... If you don't have a friend or acquaintanc who is active in politics, look up your local precinct o ward leader. ...

"In addition to specific talents which are needed (publi relations, letter writing, speaking, house-to-house calling etc.) there are two general things which desperately nee doing. One is the raising and contribution of money for th campaign. The second is the holding of small political mee ings in private homes."

You can make no more worthwhile contribution to you community and nation than to work for principles and car didates in which you believe.

"How much time do you devote to your lodge, to you church to your country club and golf course?" Senator Dirk sen once asked an audience during an address on politica responsibility. "Finally, how much time do you give you country? Doesn't it merit some of your money and you energies and some of your sacrifices?"

5. *To Run for Office.* This may strike you at first as wildl impossible. You are too busy, you lack experience, yo have no desire to "get mixed up in politics." But every states man in our history was a political amateur at one tim and most of them raised the same objections.

There is a critical need for conscientious candidates, pa ticularly on the local level where you would be most likel to start. Your party will give you the backing and th organization you need to conduct an effective campaig

Service in government may take many forms—a term on the school board—service in the state legislature—membership on a state commission—or even a career in public life.

"Conservatives have a much better record of service on voluntary, charitable, economic or cultural associations than in government," wrote Clinton Rossiter in *Conservatism in America*. This reluctance to run for public office, he adds, has worked incalculable harm on the Conservative cause.

"A moral obligation to enter the public service during the part of every qualified man's best years has become, for the generation that lies ahead, an actual necessity," David Lilienthal once declared.

Even if you do not consider it your moral obligation, run for some office at least once in your lifetime. It can be an exciting and rewarding experience.

6. *To Help Shape Conservative Programs*. Once you have the determination to battle for Conservative principles, the background information necessary to be effective, and the political involvement as a party worker or public official, you can move on to the developing of Conservative programs.

You can, as Rossiter has put it, "take honest stock of conditions in industry or society that have led to demands for special subsidies and favors, and be prepared . . . to propose remedies—countering a proposal for stiffer regulation of industry with one that would encourage self-regulation; a scheme for increased Social Security benefits with one for increased benefits AND contributions; a master plan for socialized medicine with one that is voluntary, decentralized, and self-supporting."

These programs, in general, will be based on these principles stated by Senator Tower: "The preservation of constitutional government, the responsibilities of state and local government, opposition to the concentration of power in the hands of the President, a tough foreign policy . . . and a fundamental belief and pride in the free enterprise system."

Conservatives must do more than merely counter Liberal programs. We must take the offensive by presenting our own programs first. Conservatism need not be a philosophy of opposition, and it has appeared so only because Conservatives consistently have sat idly by and let the Liberals have the first say in the Great Debate.

Where does Conservatism go from here? It goes forward, on power generated by *you* and several million other individual Conservatives, or it does not go forward at all. The Goldwaters and Byrds and Hallecks can do only so much in Congress, and the Buckleys and Moleys and Kirks can have only limited influence.

Until men who went halfway around the globe to fight for freedom in war can summon the energy to cross the street and declare for freedom in the voting booth . . . until they make up their minds to devote at least a part of their time and resources to the goal of better government . . . until every American of Conservative tendency decides to shoulder his share of the load and perhaps a little more . . . until then, Conservatism will continue to fight an uphill battle, and very probably a losing one.

A FINAL WORD

"The spark of liberty in the mind and spirit of man cannot be long extinguished," said Herbert Hoover. "It will break into flames that will destroy every coercion which seeks to limit it."

That "spark of liberty" which burns in every American breast is the chief hope of Conservatism today.

It may be depended upon to burst into indignant flame, as it has many times throughout our history, whenever government at last encroaches too far upon our individual liberties.

Flames of indignation already have broken out in opposition to federal programs which offer only more and more rigid controls as a solution to the farm problem—against proposals to solve our health problems by moving in the direction of socialized medicine—against peace programs which would have America lay down its arms and surrender its sovereignty in the fervent hope that our Cold War opponents will then be reasonable.

American liberty can be repressed only so far, even in

the pursuit of highly desirable goals. Then, history has shown, it bursts into a flame which consumes the repressive force.

We are told today that America can no longer afford its old-fashioned concepts of individual and national liberty. The technologies of production and of war, it is said, have progressed so far that individuals and nations can no longer be granted the luxury of managing their own affairs.

Certainly the reduced elbow room of the 1960s demands a social consciousness and an international concern that was never demanded of our grandfathers. But does it necessarily follow that our only course is complete submission of individual wills to the dictation of a central authority?

Conservatives say NO. They say it fervently and with a growing determination that our children will be spared the tragedy of living in an age which shall have lost the precious gift of freedom.

BIBLIOGRAPHY

American Heritage Foundation
: *Who, Me, a Politician?*, Washington, Conn., 1960

Buckley, William F., Jr.
: *Up from Liberalism*, New York, 1959

Burke, Edmund
: *An Appeal from the New to the Old Whigs*, Oxford, 1791
: *Reflections on the Revolution in France*, Oxford, 1790

Castle, Eugene W.
: *The Great Giveaway*, Chicago, 1957

Conant, James B.
: *Slums and Suburbs*, New York, 1961

Congressional Quarterly Service
: *1961-62 Current American Government*, revised, 1962.

Connery, Robert H. and Richard Leach
: *The Federal Government and Metropolitan Areas*, Cambridge, 1960

Disraeli, Benjamin
: *Whigs and Whiggism*, London, 1913

Drury, Alan
: *Advise and Consent*, Garden City, N.Y., 1959

Evans, M. Stanton
: *Revolt on the Campus*, Chicago, 1961

Flynn, John T.
: *The Road Ahead*, New York, 1949

Goldwater, Barry
: *The Conscience of a Conservative*, Shepherdsville, Ky., 1960

Hamilton, Alexander
: *Works*, New York, 1886
: *The Federalist*, Chicago, 1898

Harrison, Gordon
  Road to the Right, New York, 1954

Hayek, Peter
  The Road to Serfdom, Chicago, 1944

Hink, Heinz
  Calhoun: The Great Problem of Government (unpublished),
  1961

Hoover, Herbert
  American Individualism, New York, 1922
  The Challenge to Liberty, New York, 1934

Huxley, Aldous
  Brave New World, New York and London, 1946 (first published 1932)

Jefferson, Thomas
  The Complete Jefferson, New York, 1943

Kennedy, Robert
  The Enemy Within, New York, 1960

Kirk, Russell
  The Conservative Mind, Chicago, 1953
  A Program for Conservatives, Chicago, 1954
  Academic Freedom, Chicago, 1955

Larson, Arthur
  A Republican Looks at His Party, New York, 1956

Madison, James
  The Complete Madison, New York, 1953

Moley, Raymond
  After Seven Years, New York, 1939
  How To Keep Our Liberty, New York, 1952

Moos, Malcolm
  The Republicans, New York, 1956

New York University School of Law
  The Citizen's Participation in Public Affairs, New York, 1947

Nixon, Richard
  The Challenges We Face, New York, 1960

Prentice, H. W., Jr.
  Competitive Enterprise vs. Planned Economy, New York,
  1949

Rafferty, Max
    Suffer, Little Children, Boston, 1962

Rossiter, Clinton
    Conservatism in America, New York, 1955

Spain, August O.
    The Political Theory of John C. Calhoun, New York, 1951

Sutton, Francis X.
    The American Business Creed, Cambridge, 1956

Taft, Robert A.
    A Foreign Policy for Americans, New York, 1951

Van Riper, Paul
    Handbook of Practical Politics, New York, 1952

Wilson, Francis G.
    The American Political Mind, New York, 1949

Wood, Rob and Dean Smith
    Barry Goldwater: The Biography of a Conservative, New York, 1961

Wuerthner, J. J., Jr.
    The Businessman's Guide to Practical Politics, Chicago, 1959